nihongo notes 1
speaking and living in japan

by
osamu mizutani
nobuko mizutani

The Japan Times

ISBN4-7890-0068-0

First edition: December 1977
29th printing: December 2002

Jacket design by Koji Detake

Published by The Japan Times, Ltd.
5-4, Shibaura 4-chome, Minato-ku, Tokyo 108-0023, Japan
http://bookclub.japantimes.co.jp/

Printed in Japan

FOREWORD

This is a collection of seventy columns which first appeared in *The Japan Times* under the title of "Nihongo Notes" from August 1, 1976 to November 27, 1977, together with a list of common expressions used in daily life.

These columns are designed to explain some points that are difficult for foreigners to understand but that, once explained, can help them understand the Japanese language better. They were originally intended for those who are learning Japanese as a foreign language, but they are also useful for native speakers of Japanese in that they give them the chance to view their mother tongue in a new light.

The columns are mainly concerned with the actual usage of various common expressions rather than with their structure. We believe that, in order to communicate better in a foreign language, understanding how an expression is used and what function it performs in communication is just as important as analyzing its structure. The structural aspect of spoken Japanese is explained in *An Introduction to Modern Japanese* which was published in September this year. Reading the two books together will provide an all-around knowledge of present-day Japanese as it is actually spoken.

This book is rather small, but the wish for better communication which has prompted us to write it is large.

We would like to acknowledge the help of Janet Ashby who checked the English for these columns and offered us valuable suggestions.

November, 1977
Osamu and Nobuko Mizutani

CONTENTS

Note Concerning Romanization

The romanization used in this book (as well
as in *An Introduction to Modern Japanese*) is
based on the Hepburn system with the following
modifications.

1. When the same vowel occurs con-
   secutively, the letter is repeated rather
   than using the "‾" mark.
   ex. *Tookyoo* (instead of *Tōkyō*)
2. The sound indicated by the hiragana ん
   is written with "*n*" regardless of what
   sound follows it.
   ex. *shinbun* (instead of shimbun)
   ex. *shinpai* (instead of shimpai)

The words connected with hyphens are pronounced as one unit.
   ex. *genki-desu*
   ex. *Soo-desu-ne*

7

Dochira-e?

どちらへ

(Where are you going?)

One beautiful Sunday morning, Mr. Ernest Lerner thought he would take a walk. Just as he was leaving his house, he met the old Japanese woman who lived across the road. He immediately said *Ohayoo-gozaimasu* (Good morning) and was trying to think of other expressions he had learned when the woman suddenly asked:

Dochira-e?
どちらへ。
(Where are you going?)

Mr. Lerner was appalled. What business of hers was it where he was going? He started wondering what the Japanese equivalent of "Mind your own business" was.

Then a young man living in the neighborhood happened to pass by. He also exchanged greetings with the old woman, but when she asked him the same question he replied without hesitation:

Ee, chotto soko-made.
ええ、ちょっと　そこまで。
(Oh, just down the street.)

8

Upon hearing this exchange Mr. Lerner suddenly realized that he needn't have been specific in answering the woman's question. From then on he followed the young man's example when greeting the woman.

*   *   *

When a Japanese asks *Dochira-e?* he is not trying to be nosey. The feeling behind this greeting is that the speaker is happy that you are healthy and well-off enough to go out and have a good time, or he is worried that you have to be so busy as to go out.

In any case, this question simply shows that he is concerned about your well-being, and Japanese use it in the same way that English-speaking people never fail to ask "How are you?" whenever they meet someone they know.

Iie

いいえ

(No!)

After a hot day's work, Mr. Ernest Lerner was having some beer with Mr. Yasuda, a Japanese acquaintance. Mr. Yasuda always had been a modest, pleasant person, but that evening Mr. Lerner felt somewhat irritated that Mr. Yasuda was being too agreeable. He kept saying *Ee, ee* or, *Ee, soo-desu-ne*, to whatever Mr. Lerner thought. Mr. Lerner began wondering if this gentleman ever had the word *Iie* in his vocabulary.

When it was almost time to part, Mr. Lerner noticed that Mr. Yasuda had a very stylish, brand-new watch, and complimented him on it. Mr. Yasuda instantly replied,

Iie, sonna koto-wa arimasen.
いいえ、そんな ことは ありません。
(No, it's no such thing!)

Mr. Lerner was surprised by his unusually decisive tone, and looked him in the face. Then Mr. Yasuda quickly added,

Yasumono-desu-yo, konnano.
(Just cheap stuff.)

*   *   *

10

Some Westerners wonder why Japanese hate to say *lie* and resort to almost every possible measure to avoid saying it, but there *are* situations when Japanese positively say *lie*. What are those situations?

Japanese have in their minds what might be called psychological difficulty in denying what other people think or wish. Saying "No" to someone's opinion or request seems to them like denying him as a human being and consequently destroying a good relationship with him.

When saying "No" does not involve any possibility of hurting someone or endangering the good relationship, Japanese feel free to say "No." To such a question as "Is this the right way to the station?" they say *lie* or *lie, chigaimasu* (*lit.* No, it's different.) quite readily.

The situation with the watch described above is the one when Japanese can most happily say *lie* because denying one's own superiority can help strengthen a good relationship. In the same way, Japanese are quite positive in denying what the other person thinks is his weak point. If you want to hear your Japanese acquaintances say *lie, sonna koto-wa arimasen*, try saying that your Japanese hasn't improved a bit since last year or that you're getting old and weak.

Nomitai-desu-ka

のみたいですか

(Do you want to drink it?)

Professor Takahashi, who lived a few doors away, visited Mr. Ernest Lerner one afternoon. Mr. Lerner wanted to serve him a cup of tea, and asked, meaning "Would you like to have some tea?":

Ocha-o nomitai-desu-ka.
(Do you want to drink some tea?)

Prof. Takahashi said *Iie* (No) rather bluntly.
Since his guest was much older, Mr. Lerner thought he should have spoken more politely, and he tried asking the same question again using very polite phrasing.

Ocha-o onomi-ni naritai-desu-ka.

To this painstaking courtesy, Prof. Takahashi still did not respond too warmly, and the conversation after that did not go smoothly. It seemed as if Mr. Lerner had made his offer in the wrong way.

*   *   *

Some people will say Mr. Lerner should have said.

Ocha-demo ikaga-desu-ka.
お茶でも　いかがですか。

(Would you care for a cup of tea?)

Some people will say he should have served tea without asking. In any case, the trouble seems to be with the word *nomitai*.

Tai, the last part of *nomitai*, means "want to." It is not used, however, to ask someone else's wish when politeness is required. Japanese feel that a person's wish is purely a private matter, and that it is improper, not only impolite, to ask about it directly.

To be polite, in any language, there are things one can talk about and things one shouldn't; asking someone else's wish is considered to be the latter in Japan.

It is quite different among Westerners, especially English-speaking people. Some Westerners complain that Japanese often go ahead and put sugar and cream in the tea or coffee of their guests without first asking. Some Japanese, on the other hand, feel embarrassed when asked exactly in what way they would like their beverage to be prepared.

To ask or not to ask, that seems to be the question, but the question can be resolved if the people on both sides are prepared for either way of politeness.

Aizuchi

あいづち

(How Japanese listen)

Mr. Ernest Lerner wanted to tell Mrs. Matsumoto, his landlady, about his recent trip. When he finished the first phrase, *Senshuu umi-e ittara* (When I went to the sea last week), Mrs. Matsumoto immediately said,

> *Ee, ee.*
> ええ、ええ。
> (Yes, yes.)

Mr. Lerner was somewhat surprised by this unexpected response, but tried to continue. He said, *mizu-wa kiree-datta-n-desu-ga* (the water was clean, but), then again Mrs. Matsumoto said,

> *Soo-desu-ka.*
> そうですか。
> (Is that so?)

Mr. Lerner almost screamed, *hito-ga oozee-de* (there were so many people), and Mrs. Matsumoto agreed,

> *Soo-deshoo-ne.*
> そうでしょうね。

14

(It must be so.)

In this way Mrs. Matsumoto kept throwing in short answers until Mr. Lerner felt that his Japanese was so poor that she did not want to listen to him, and he cut the conversation short.

* * *

Short answers such as *Hai*, *Ee*, *Soo-desu-ka*, *Soo-deshoo-ne*, which are called *aizuchi* are used as a signal to show that the listener is listening attentively and wants the speaker to go on. Japanese feel uneasy when the listener remains silent without giving *aizuchi*.

Japanese believe, in most cases unconsciously, that a flow of speech is made up not only by the speaker but also by the listener who participates by giving *aizuchi*. Sometimes the listener goes so far as to finish up what the speaker is going to say. Two people, A and B, for example, join together in making up one flow of speech; this might be illustrated as ———_———
—_———_———_.

This is quite different from the Western notion of what conversation should be like. Westerners consider it good manners to keep silent without interrupting the speaker while he is speaking.

Konnichiwa

こんにちは

(Good afternoon)

Mr. Ernest Lerner went to his office late one day. It was almost two in the afternoon so he said, instead of *Ohayoo-gozaimasu* (Good morning),

Konnichiwa
こんにちは。
(Good afternoon)

There were several people working in the office. All of them turned to him, but they did not say anything for a moment; then some of them said *Konnichiwa* hesitantly; others just nodded silently.

Mr. Lerner did not understand. Why did *Konnichiwa* sound strange? Isn't it a perfectly reasonable greeting, corresponding to English greetings such as "Good morning," "Good day," or "Hello"?

*　　　*　　　*

As far as the hour of the day is concerned, it is proper to say *Konnichiwa* at two in the afternoon, but it is not appropriate to say it to one's colleagues.

Among the several greetings exchanged when

16

meeting people, *Ohayoo-gozaimasu* can be used to any person, to people in any relationship with you, but the situations where *Konnichiwa* and *Konbanwa* (Good evening) can be used are rather limited. These two are used with people who do not belong to one's own group.

Needless to say, they cannot be used among family members. People working at the same office are usually considered to be members of one's own group, though people's conception of the size or content of this group varies according to the individual.

The people at Mr. Lerner's office regarded him as a member of their group; which is why they were embarrassed to be greeted by him with *Konnichiwa*. If they had regarded him as an outsider, they would have accepted it as a matter of fact.

One more thing about *Konnichiwa* and *Konbanwa* is that they do not sound very polite and cannot be used to greet one's superiors. For example, a customer greets a clerk at the store with *Konnichiwa* or *Konbanwa*, but the clerk does not return the same greeting; he usually says *Irasshaimase* (*lit.* I'm glad you have come).

When Japanese feel *Konnichiwa* or *Konbanwa* to be inappropriate, they turn to various substitutes, among which referring to the climate is a very popular one; they often greet others by saying that it is very cold, or hot, or that it has been raining a great deal.

Raishawaa-San

ライシャワーさん

(Mr. Reischauer)

Mr. Ernest Lerner likes to use *-san,* a Japanese term of respect; it can stand for Mr., Mrs., and Miss, and it can be attached to first names as well as last names. It is less discriminatory than English terms which distinguish male from female, and married woman from unmarried, though recently many women are beginning to prefer Ms.

The other day, when Mr. Lerner referred to Prof. Reischauer, he said

> *Raishawaa-san*
> ライシャワーさん。
> (Mr. Reischauer).

Miss Yoshida, one of the listeners at that time, interrupted him and asked if he knew the former ambassador personally. He said no, and wanted to ask her why she had raised that question, but the conversation went on too rapidly and he did not have the chance to do so.

*   *   *

As Mr. Lerner feels, *-san* is a very convenient suffix. It is added not only to people's names, but also to the names of occupations such as *omawari-san* (policeman), *yuubin'ya-san* (mailman), *nikuya-san* (butcher), and *untenshu-san* (driver).

The Japanese also use *-san* in various types of relationships such as *okyaku-san* (customer) and *otonari-san* (people living next door). Why not *Raishawaa-san*?

The former ambassador to Japan is certainly a person worthy of respect, but he is usually called without *-san* in Japanese. Not only he but also great Japanese statesmen and outstanding people in academic fields are deprived of *-san*, unless they are personal acquaintances of the speaker. *San* does not show respect only; it also indicates intimacy.

The infamous as well as the famous are also deprived of *-san*. The only exception is if you want to make people laugh you can say *dorooboo-san* (Mr. Thief), *obake-san* (Mr. Monster), or *kichigai-san* (Mr. Loony).

San has one more peculiarity about which you should be careful. It cannot be used with one's own name or the names of one's family members. In English, people sometimes add Mr., Mrs. or Miss to their own names and say "This is Mr. Jones speaking," or "I'm Mrs. Smith." But in Japanese you have to be very careful not to add *-san* to your own name, and particularly not to the name of your wife when referring to her.

Gurai, hodo, bakari

ぐらい、ほど、ばかり

(About, approximately, nearly)

At a little grocery store in the neighborhood Mr. Ernest Lerner was taking some time deciding what fruit to buy, when a woman came in and asked for some pears. When the shopkeeper asked how many she wanted, she said,

Soo-ne, mittsu-gurai.
そうね、みっつぐらい。
(Well, about three of them.)

The shopkeeper picked up three pears and gave them to her. Then another woman came in and asked for apples, saying *yottsu-hodo* (about four).

Mr. Lerner was reminded of what he had observed at the office a few days before. Mr. Takada asked Miss Saito to lend him *sen-yen-bakari* (about ¥1,000). Mr. Lerner wondered if Miss Saito would give him ¥999 or ¥1,001 since she was asked for about ¥1,000. But she merely handed him one ¥1,000 bill, completely ignoring the word *bakari*.

English-speaking people also use such expressions as "about twenty" "a few," or "several," but it seems to many Westerners that Japanese actually dislike giving exact numbers.

*　　　*　　　*

The use of such expressions as *gurai*, *hodo*, and *bakari* shows that the speaker does not want to press the listener by demanding an exact amount. Rather he wants to make the listener comfortable by leaving him some margin for choice. Suppose your friend happened to have only ¥999 to spare when you asked for ¥1,000; he would be embarrassed since he does not want to refuse your request. Although this is a hypothetical example, the underlying idea is such consideration toward others.

Recently this usage, like other aspects of Japanese, is undergoing some change. Young people tend to discard it, feeling that it is meaningless to try to make one's requests vague — if the listener finds your request inconvenient, he can just say so.

However, you will notice in your life here that most Japanese still use *gurai*, *hodo*, and *bakari* very often, perhaps more often than they realize.

Doomo

どうも

(Indeed)

One word that bothers Mr. Ernest Lerner now is *doomo*. English-Japanese dictionaries give "indeed" and "somehow" as definitions for it, but he suspects that its actual usage covers a much wider range.

The people at his office, for instance, use *doomo* for many other purposes. They say *Kinoo-wa, doomo* (*lit.* Indeed yesterday) when they meet; they say just *Doomo* to thank others and to apologize. They also say *Ja, doomo* when they part.

Doomo is used to cut answers short, too. When Mr. Lerner asked Mr. Takada how his study of English was going, he said *Doomo-nee*. He did not mean that his English had made great progress; he meant just the opposite.

Probably most Japanese do not realize how often they use, or overuse, this word. *Doomo* literally means "in all ways," or "no matter how I look at it." Actually it is used to mean various things. There are two very common uses of *doomo* — as a social expression and as an indication of negative judgment.

As a social expression it is used by itself to mean "Thank you," "Sorry," "Excuse me,"

22

"Thank you for coming," "Sorry to take your time," to mention just a few. The last two are equivalent to "Hello" and "Good-bye" respectively. In these expressions the part that follows *doomo* is left out; for example in the case of *Doomo arigatoo-gozaimasu*, *arigatoo-gozaimasu* is understood.

The second usage is also very common. If you ask someone a question and he just says *Watashi-wa doomo. . .* (*lit.* I somehow. . .) in a hesitant tone, he means that he does not know the answer. Or if you ask someone's opinion about something and the reply is *Doomo. . .* or *Doomo-nee*, it means that he feels negatively about it; Mr. Takada used *doomo* in this way when Mr. Lerner asked him about his study of English.

Doomo changes its meaning depending not only on the situation but also on the tone in which it is spoken. If you pronounce it quickly, it sounds casual. (Some people say *Doomo, doomo* quickly in greeting people; this sounds very casual and cannot be used when you want to be polite or formal.) But if you pronounce it slowly, it sounds sincere and polite. In stating negative judgment, it is pronounced in a hesitant, dangling tone.

Ikaga-desu-ka

いかがですか

(How are you?)

Mr. Lerner caught a bad cold and had to stay home for about a week. When he recovered and returned to the office, Miss Yoshida came up to him and said,

Ikaga-desu-ka.
いかがですか。
(How are you?)

This surprised Mr. Lerner because it was the first time anyone had asked him this question. It may be hard to believe, but this expression, which most students of Japanese learn at an early stage as the equivalent of "How are you?" is actually used very seldom. Mr. Lerner still remembers how puzzled his Japanese friend looked when he greeted him with *Ikaga-desu-ka*; he thought that he must have been being too formal and tried *Doo-desu-ka* next time, but still did not get the kind of response he had hoped for.

*   *   *

To Japanese, it is strange to say *Ikaga-desu-ka* or *Doo-desu-ka* to someone they meet every day. These kinds of questions are asked only when the two people have not met for a long time

24

or when someone has had an unfortunate experience or an important change in his life. In fact, it is not the Japanese custom to ask someone how he is as a form of greeting. To put it more strongly, they feel it inappropriate and even bad manners to ask others such a personal question unless they are close friends.

Then how do the Japanese greet each other? There are various ways. Referring to the weather is certainly one of them. To share happiness in having good weather and worry about bad weather confirms the good relations between the speaker and the listener.

Another way of greetings is to express thanks for the kindness the speaker received the last time they met or to apologize for his rudeness. This explains why *Doomo* can be used in place of "Hello."

And one more way is to ask someone where he is going. The exchange of *Dochira-e?* (or *Odekake-desu-ka*) and *Chotto soko-made* thus actually corresponds to "How are you?" and "Fine, thanks."

From the viewpoint of actual usage these greetings might be translated as:

Dochira-e? (*lit.* Where are you going?)
—Hello, how are you?
Chotto soko-made. (*lit.* Just down the street.) — Fine, thanks. And you?
Ja, itte-rasshai. (*lit.* Go and come back.)
—I'm fine, too. Have a good time.

Hai, orimasu-kedo. . .

はい、おりますけど……

(Yes, he's home, but. . .)

Mr. Lerner called Mr. Takahashi's home, and Mrs. Takahashi answered the phone. When he asked her if her husband was home, she said,

Hai, orimasu-kedo. . .
はい、おりますけど……
(Yes, he's home, but. . .)

Mr. Lerner thought that she was going to say that her husband was busy and could not talk on the phone or something similar after the word *kedo*, "but," and waited for her to finish her sentence. However, she seemed to be waiting for him to speak, so he went ahead and asked her if he could talk to Mr. Takahashi. She said yes and immediately brought her husband to the phone.

Mr. Lerner has noticed that Japanese seem to like to leave their sentences unfinished in this way, often ending their phrases with *kedo* or *ga*, which both mean "but." Just a couple of days earlier, when he asked for a Mr. Saito among the several gentlemen present, Mr. Saito stood and said,

Watashi-desu-ga. . .

(I am Mr. Saito, but. . .)

*   *   *

Kedo or *ga* (*kedo* is more colloquial than *ga*) used in the above examples do not mean "on the contrary." The English "but" can also be used in a similar way in such expressions as "Excuse me, but aren't you Mr. Lerner?" or "Sorry to trouble you, but could you tell me how to get to Ginza?"

The difference between *kedo* or *ga* and "but" is that the former is used much more frequently and that the part following it is very often understood and not said out loud.

The part that is understood is usually an inquiry about the listener's wishes. For example, after *Hai, orimasu-kedo*, the part meaning "Shall I call him for you?" is left out; and after *Watashi-desu-ga*, "What can I do for you?" is understood. When used for this purpose, *ga* or *kedo* is pronounced in a hesitant, dangling tone so that it does not sound final.

In fact, *kedo* or *ga* is used to encourage the listener to go ahead and make a request.

This is connected to the Japanese notion that conversation is a flow of speech made up by two people, the speaker and the listener, rather than by the speaker alone. It is therefore polite and considerate, in Japanese, to leave one's sentences unfinished for the listener to complete.

Anata

あなた

(You)

Mr. Lerner was talking with Mr. Yamamoto, the director of his company. When he said:

Anata-mo ikimasu-ka.
あなたも　いきますか。
(Are you going, too?)

Mr. Yamamoto did not reply for a moment. He looked at Mr. Lerner and then said "yes" coldly. Afterward, Mr. Takada, who was present then, told Mr. Lerner that it was not polite to call the director *anata*.

After this, Mr. Lerner paid careful attention to how *anata* is used by Japanese, and found it to be rather unpopular among them. It was surprising to learn how infrequently it is used compared with "you," its apparent English equivalent.

*　　　*　　　*

The Japanese very often do without any personal pronouns; indeed Japanese seem to avoid using them. When they have to use some word to refer to a person, they use personal names instead of the personal pronouns corresponding to "he," "she," or "you" in English. It is sometimes impossible to judge whether the speaker is

28

talking about the second or third person from just looking at the sentence itself. For example, *Yamamoto-san-mo ikimasu-ka* literally means "Is Mr. Yamamoto going, too?" but in practice it can mean "Are you going, too?"

Sometimes the names of positions are used instead of personal names. Such terms as *sensee* (teacher), *shachoo* (director), *okusan* (wife) and *okaasan* (mother) are used in place of the name or *anata*. Especially when the position deserves respect, its name should be used rather than the personal name or *anata*. Thus Mr. Lerner should have said *Shachoo-mo irasshaimasu-ka* to his director instead of *Anata-mo ikimasu-ka*. (The verb must be chosen according to the level of politeness, so *irasshaimasu* is used instead of *ikimasu*.)

Anata is used in a very limited way. It can be used by older people to younger people. A teacher can call his student *anata*, but a student should not call his teacher *anata*. A mother can say *Anata-mo iku?* to her child (*Iku* is the non-polite form of *ikimasu*), but the child never uses the same sentence to his mother.

Anata is also used among women of the same age. (Men use *kimi* or *omae* in the same situation.) Here, too, the vulnerable *anata* is liable to be replaced by personal names or the names of positions. Two housewives are very likely to say,

A: *Okusan-mo iku?* (*lit.* Is the wife going, too?)
B: *Ee, okusan-mo?* (*lit.* Yes. The wife, too?)

This exchange actually means "Are you going, too?" and "Yes. You, too?"

Shitsuree-shimasu

失礼します

(Excuse me)

The other day Mr. Yasuda came to see Mr. Lerner at his office to discuss some business. Before entering the office, he stopped at the door and said,

(1) *Shitsuree-shimasu.*
　　　失礼します。
This literally means "I'm going to be rude (enough to enter the office)."

When he approached Mr. Lerner, he bowed and said,

(2) *Senjitsu-wa shitsuree-shimashita*
which literally means "I was rude the other day (when we met)."

When Mr. Lerner asked him to sit down, he said,

(3) *Shitsuree-shimasu*
meaning "I'm going to be rude (enough to sit down)."

When he left, he said,

(4) *Doomo shitsuree-shimashita*
or, "I have been rude (enough to take your time.

Now I'm leaving).''

These four *shitsuree*s mean respectively (1) Excuse me, (2) Hello, how are you? (3) Thank you and (4) Good-bye.

*   *   *

The word *shitsuree* itself means rudeness; *shitsuree-shimasu* literally means ''I'm going to do something rude. Please excuse me,'' and *shitsuree-shimashita* literally means ''I have been rude to you. Please forgive me.'' Both *shitsuree-shimasu* and *shitsuree-shimashita* are actually used to express gratitude as well as apology, and even to say good-bye. Similarly, other expressions such as *osoreirimasu*, *sumimasen*, and *warui-ne* (*lit.* It's bad) are also used for both apology and gratitude.

Japanese may seem to be apologizing all the time, and this custom might irritate foreigners as being overly formal or even hypocritical. But Japanese themselves do not think that they are using the same expression for different purposes; to their mind, to apologize for being rude and to thank someone for his kindness are not two different things, but rather something like two sides of a coin.

Therefore, we would like to conclude this short article by saying,

Shitsuree-shimashita.
失礼しました。
(Thank you very much for reading it. We're sorry we took your time.)

31

Motte-kimasu

もってきます

(I'll bring it)

When Mr. Lerner asked Miss Yoshida, who works at the same company, to tell him a little bit about Kabuki, she offered to show him a book she had, saying,

Ashita motte-kimasu.
あした　もってきます。
(I'll bring it tomorrow.)

The next day, she brought the book and showed it to Mr. Lerner, but he still had some questions which she couldn't answer. She remarked that her brother could easily answer those questions, Mr. Lerner said,

Ja, kondo otooto-san-o motte-kite-kudasai.
(Then bring your brother next time.)

Everybody burst out laughing, and Miss Yoshida said it was the cutest joke she had ever heard.

But Mr. Lerner had not meant to make a joke. He had simply translated the English verb 'to bring' as *motte-kuru*.

*   *   *

Some people might be reminded here of the distinction between *iru* and *aru* (both "to be"). The verb *iru* is used for living things while the verb *aru* is used with inanimate things; for example, *hito-ga imasu* means "there is a person" and *hon-ga arimasu* is used for "there is a book."

The verb *motte-kuru* is used for bringing inanimate things such as books, while *tsurete-kuru* is used for bringing persons or other living things. Nobody would have laughed if Mr. Lerner had said,

Otooto-san-o tsurete-kite-kudasai.
おとうとさんを　つれてきてください。
(Bring your brother.)

In the case of *iru* and *aru*, the distinction is very rigid; all inanimate things are referred to with *aru*, and all living things are referred to with the verb *iru*, from human beings down to such tiny creatures as mosquitoes.

The distinction between *tsurete-kuru* and *motte-kuru* is somewhat different. *Motte-kuru* is used in the case of all inanimate things, but *tsurete-kuru* is not necessarily used with all living things. Human beings are described with this verb, and for dogs, too, it is used without question; but for smaller pets like goldfish or birds, one does not usually use *tsurete-kuru*. It seems that *tsurete-kuru* presupposes that the object of the action is capable of moving, guided by the person who does the action of bringing it. Human beings, however, do not have to possess this characteristic in order to be described with *tsurete-kuru* — bringing a baby is described as *tsurete-kuru* even though he cannot walk yet.

Yaseru hito?

やせる人

(A Person who is getting thinner?)

While several people were leisurely talking during their coffee break, Mr. Lerner mentioned that he drinks beer every day. Mr. Takada asked him when he drinks it, and Mr. Lerner answered that he drinks it when he returns home. He used the phrase,

> *Uchi-e kaeru toki*
> うちへ　かえる　とき
> (When I return home).

Then Mr. Takada asked where he drinks. Mr. Lerner was puzzled but replied that of course it was at home. This time Mr. Takada looked puzzled, and seemed to want further explanation, but the coffee break was over so the discussion had to be stopped.

*　　　*　　　*

To say that you like to have a glass of beer "when you return home," you have to say *uchi-e kaetta toki*, instead of saying *uchi-e kaeru toki*. (*Kaetta* is the past tense of *kaeru*.) Since the verb *kaeru* actually refers to the process of going home rather than reaching home, *uchi-e kaeru toki* means "when you are on your way home."

34

That is why Mr. Takada was curious to know at what bar Mr. Lerner was drinking.

Kaetta toki actually means "when you have completed the action of going home," so you can say

Uchi-e kaetta toki biiru-o nomimasu.
うちへ　かえった　とき　ビールを　のみます。

to mean that you drink beer when you are at home.

To express that some action has been completed, you have to use verbs in the past tense. *Kekkon-suru hito* means a person who is going to get married, while *kekkon-shita hito* refers to someone who has already gotten married.

Similarly the past tense of the verb *yaseru*, "to become thin," is used in modifying a person, *yaseta hito*. If you say *yaseru hito*, it gives the unlikely picture of a person who is getting thinner and thinner before your very eyes.

Kaetta, *kekkon-shita*, *yaseta*, these can be called the past forms, but the Japanese idea of the past is quite different from that of English-speakers.

Soo-desu-ne. Soo-desu-yo.

そうですね。そうですよ。

(That's right. That's right.)

Mr. Lerner got tired of saying *Soo-desu-ne* all the time to show agreement. Since *Soo-desu-yo* seemed to mean the same thing, he thought he would try using it instead.

One morning in front of the station, he met Mr. Okada, who said with a smile, *Hayai-desu-ne* (You're early).

Instead of saying *Soo-desu-ne,* Mr. Lerner said *Soo-desu-yo.* Mr. Okada looked a little surprised and then said, *Samuku narimashita-ne* (It has become cold). Since Mr. Lerner wanted to strongly emphasize his agreement, he said loudly,

Ee, soo-desu-yo.
ええ、そうですよ。

Mr. Okada did not talk much during the ride on the train that morning. Mr. Lerner suspected that the shift from *-ne* to *-yo* had produced some bad effect.

*   *   *

There is a great difference between *-yo* and *-ne*, and using *-yo* in the wrong way can be quite damaging to good relations with your Japanese friends and acquaintances.

Ne is used to show your own agreement and your expectation that the listener will agree with you. Thus greetings which refer to the weather always end in *-ne* because they are exchanged to create a feeling of oneness between two people.

On the other hand, *-yo* is used to emphatically state your own judgment, regardless of what the listener might think. It is often used to tell someone information he should know or to tell him what he should do. Mothers say *Moo hachiji desu-yo* (It's already eight o'clock!) or *Moo osoi-desu-yo* (It's getting late!) to urge their children to hurry. Thus you have to be careful not to overuse *yo*; otherwise you might impress others as an aggressive, patronizing speaker.

However *-yo* should be used to encourage the listener by denying his uneasiness or his lack of confidence. *Sonna koto-wa arimasen-yo* (That's not so) is the appropriate answer to such statements as "I'm poor at this," or "I don't have any talent for this." Doctors say *Daijoobu-desu-yo* (Don't worry) to a nervous patient before his surgical operation. In this usage also, *-yo* should not be used too much when speaking to your superiors.

No other words are so short and yet so significant as *-ne* and *-yo*.

Ki-o tsukenakucha ikemasen-ne.
(We should be careful, shouldn't we?)
Ki-o tsukenakucha ikemasen-yo.
(You should be careful, I tell you.)

Kaette-kudasai

かえってください

(Please go home)

Last Saturday Mr. Takada came to visit Mr. Lerner. The two had a very good time together, and when Mr. Takada left, Mr. Lerner really wished to have him come again, so he said,

Sugu kaette-kudasai.

meaning "Please come back soon."

Mr. Takada looked astonished, remained silent for a while, and then burst out laughing. He knew English well enough to understand why this mistake happened; to come back means to come again, and Mr. Lerner directly translated "come back" as *kaeru.*

When Mr. Takada explained that *Kaette-kudasai* means "Please go home," Mr. Lerner could not laugh. He was afraid that he had made the same mistake before.

*   *   *

The verb *kaeru* does not mean "to come back to the place where one is now." It means "to go back to the place where one belongs." Usually one's home is where one belongs; therefore, *kaerimasu* means "I'm going home" and *Kaette-*

38

kudasai means "Please go home." If you want your visitor to come again, you have to say,

Mata kite-kudasai.
また　来てください。
(Please come again.)

Places other than one's home can be where one belongs, too. One's job can be where one belongs, depending on how one feels about it. Also, in the case of inhabitants in big cities who are from the country, they often feel their hometown is where they belong. So they say *kuni-e kaerimasu* when they visit their parents in the country.

A friend's house or a store is not usually where you belong. When you are visiting someone for a few hours, or buying things at a store and leave for a short while, you should say *modotte-kimasu*. If you say to a storekeeper *kaerimasu* when you intend to come back after getting some money at the bank or after making a telephone call, he may think you gave up and went home and end up selling what you want to buy. You can ask him to save something for you by saying,

Sugu modotte-kimasu-kara totte-oite-kudasai.

(I'll be back soon, so please save this for me.)

39

Aa, are-desu-ka

ああ、あれですか

(Oh, is it that?)

One afternoon Miss Yoshida came to Mr. Lerner and asked if he could join the picnic she was planning. While she was explaining her plan, Mr. Takada passed by and asked what she was talking about. She said,

Are-desu.
あれです。
(About that. — *lit.* It is that.)

Then Mr. Takada said,

Aa, are-desu-ka.
ああ、あれですか。
(Oh, about that? — *lit.* Oh, is it that?)

She never mentioned the picnic or her plan in this exchange, but he immediately . understood anyway.

*　　　*　　　*

Such words as *kore* "this," *sore* "that," *are* "that over there," and *dore* "which one" are used to point out things the speaker wants to refer to. Most textbooks explain that *kore* is used to refer to things close to the speaker and *sore* to things close to the listener, and *are* is used to refer to things far from both the speaker and the listener. This explanation is correct so far as the question of space is concerned, but you must keep in mind that the relation between the speaker and the listener and the thing referred to is even more important than the physical distance between the speaker and the thing he refers to.

For instance, *are* presupposes that the speaker and the listener share a knowledge of the subject matter. When the listener has no knowledge of the subject matter, *sore* is used instead of *are*.

The knowledge of the subject matter does not have to be acquired through sight. When someone hears a strange noise outside the room, he says to a person in the same room *Are-wa nan-desu-ka* (What is that?) because both the speaker and the listener have heard the noise and thereby acquired a common knowledge of it.

The knowledge does not have to be gained through personal experience, either. The picture of Mona Liza is usually referred to as *are* even if the speaker or the listener have not seen it because it is known to both of them. But if you talk about some picture unknown to the listener, *sore* is used.

Since how often *are* is used roughly corresponds to the amount of knowledge the speaker and the listener share, you will hear it more often among family members and among co-workers. Couples who have been married a long time naturally tend to use it quite often. A happily married husband is very likely to say to his wife,

Are-o motte-kite.
あれを　持ってきて。
(Bring me that.)

And she will bring exactly what he wants.

41

Shujin = Shuujin?

主人 = 囚人?

(Husband = Prisoner?)

The other day Mr. Takada introduced his sister Michiko to Mr. Lerner. When Mr. Lerner asked her if she had a job she answered that she was so busy taking care of her husband and child that she could not think of going out to work. Mr. Lerner expressed his sympathy by saying,

Shuufu-wa taihen-desu-ne. He meant "being a housewife is really hard," but both Michiko and Mr. Takada looked puzzled and were silent. Mr. Lerner added,

Nihon-no shuujin-wa amari tetsudaimasen-kara-ne, meaning "Japanese husbands do not help their wives very much."

Then Mr. Takada realized that Mr. Lerner had made a mistake in pronunciation and explained. Mr. Lerner had said *shuufu* (ugly woman) for *shufu* (housewife), and *shuujin* (prisoner) for *shujin* (husband). The slight mistake in pronouncing the *shu* sound had produced a grim picture of a household made up of a prisoner and an ugly woman.

*　　　*　　　*

Except for a few points, the pronunciation of Japanese is rather easy for an English speaking person. One point is that the Japanese (as seen in

42

katakana and *hiragana*) pronounce each syllable or sound unit with approximately the same length, regard a short vowel and a long vowel as two different sound units, and also regard the ひ sound as a separate sound unit. Thus the word *shujin* (husband) is made up of three sound units — *shu*, *ji*, and *n*, while *shuujin* (prisoner) is made up of four — *shu*, *u*, *ji*, and *n*. Thus in the Japanese notion the difference between *shujin* and *shuujin* is not in the length of the *u* sound but it is in the number of sound units included.

Shujin (husband)　主人　　しゆ　じ　ん

Shuujin (prisoner)　囚人　　しゆ　う　じ　ん

Unlike English the length of the vowel can make a difference in meaning, so English speakers need to be especially careful with vowel length in Japanese. Some important word pairs are found among family terms. For instance, *ojisan* means "uncle" or "older man" and *ojiisan* means "grandfather" or "old man," while *obasan* means "aunt" or "older woman" and *obaasan* means "grandmother" or "old woman."

It may help to practice by saying the following pairs:

yume (dream) — *yuumee* (famous)

koi (love) — *kooi* (kindness)

oya (parent) — *ooya* (landlord)

chizu (map) — *chiizu* (cheese)

Ohara (name) 小原 — *Oohara* (name) 大原

Akanboo-ni nakareta

赤ん坊に　泣かれた

(I was cried by the baby!)

Since Mr. Okada looked all tired out, Mr. Lerner asked if he was ill. Mr. Okada said no and explained that he had not slept very well the night before. He added.

Akanboo-ni nakareta-node.
(Because the baby cried.)

The word *nakareta* was new to Mr. Lerner. The past form of the verb *naku* "to cry" should be *naita*. He had learned that verbs ending in *-areru* (present) or *-areta* (past) are used to express politeness, but it seemed strange to use a polite term when talking about one's own baby.

Mr. Takada explained that *nakareta* is the passive form of *naita*. Trying to help him understand. Mr. Takada gave another example of the passive, *Kanai-ni byooki-ni narareta* (My wife became ill). This puzzled Mr. Lerner even more. Why is the passive form used here?

*　　　*　　　*

The passive form in Japanese can be used the same as in English but can also be used in a quite different way as seen above. The idea is that when the speaker is affected by an action done by someone else, the passive form is used. The action does not have to involve two agents, doer and receiver, as long as it affects the speaker. Thus when the rainfall causes the speaker some trouble, he says *Ame-ni furareta* (I was inconvenienced by the rain) rather than saying *Ame-ga futta* (It rained); when someone's death affects the speaker, he says *Ano-hito-ni shinareta* (He died on me) instead of saying *Ano-hito-ga shinda* (He died).

Thus the same thing can be expressed differently depending on how the speaker feels about it. When a baby cries during the night, a loving mother will say,

Akachan-ga naita.
赤ちゃんが　泣いた。
(The baby cried,

while a father who has to get up early and go to work will naturally say,

Akanboo-ni nakareta.
赤ん坊に　泣かれた。
(I suffered from the baby's crying.)

Senjitsu-wa gochisoosama-deshita

先日は　ごちそうさまでした

(Thank you for the treat the other day)

The other day Mr. Lerner met Mr. Saito after about two months. Mr. Saito greeted him by saying,

Senjitsu-wa gochisoosama-deshita.
(Thank you for the treat the other day.)

Mr. Lerner was surprised that Mr. Saito referred to their previous meeting that had taken place quite a while before; and he was even more surprised when he remembered that he had only bought him a cup of coffee at a coffee shop. It did not seem to be worth Mr. Saito's expressing gratitude again after two months.

But when he started thinking about it, he realized that almost everyone said the same thing as Mr. Saito had. He could not help wondering if one has to have a good memory in order to be polite in Japan.

*　　　*　　　*

The answer to Mr. Lerner's question is yes. A Japanese has to remember and express gratitude for the favors received at the last meeting. You might think it is not necessary because you already thanked him adequately at the time, but

46

it is customary to do so in Japan and is bad manners not to do so.

This custom may give you the impression that Japanese are overly conscious of the money they spend to treat others, but that is not the case. It is important to remember your meeting and having a good time together rather than who treated whom. You should refer to the previous meeting even when there was no giving and receiving of favors; in such cases you are supposed to say

Senjitsu-wa shitsuree-shimashita.
先日は　失礼しました。
(I was rude the last time we met.)

instead of *Senjitsu-wa gochisoosama-deshita.* What really counts is to show that you and the listener remember sharing the same experience; the memory of having the same experience helps to establish good relations between the two of you. Japanese consider it essential to start by establishing good relations before getting down to business. That is why this expression is used as a greeting when an English-speaking person would say "How have you been?" or just "Hello."

We have heard quite a few Japanese complain that their American acquaintances do not follow this custom: some of them even think it is rude.

Koko-de tomete-kudasai

ここで　とめてください

(Please stop here)

One afternoon Mr. Lerner went out with Mr. Takada on business. When the taxi they took reached their destination, Mr. Lerner said,

Koko-de tomete-kudasai.
(Please stop here.)

After they got out Mr. Takada asked if Mr. Lerner was angry at the way the taxi driver had talked. Mr. Lerner did not understand why Mr. Takada asked this question because he had not paid any particular attention to it. Mr. Takada explained that Mr. Lerner had sounded very angry when he asked the driver to stop.

*　　　*　　　*

Koko-de tomete-kudasai is a correct Japanese sentence, appropriate in the situation in which Mr. Lerner used it. It was not the words themselves but the tone that caused a misunderstanding. He pronounced the last part of the sentence, *tomete-kudasai*, clearly and strongly, as is natural for a native speaker of English. But a Japanese would not say it that way; he would say the last part of the sentence softly and with a falling tone. *Tomete-kudasai* is understood in this situation — the driver knew that it was about time to stop — so it should be pronounced softly, while *Koko-de* conveys important information and therefore should be said more clearly and strongly than *tomete-kudasai.*

Thus, it should be

KOKO-DE tomete-kudasai.
ここで　とめてください。

instead of

Koko-de TOMETE-KUDASAI.
ここで　とめてください。

If you put the stress on *tomete-kudasai,* it will sound as if you are irritated with the driver.

In the same way, when you ask for someone on the phone you should say

YAMADA-SAN-O onegai-shimasu.
(I'd like to speak to Mr. Yamada)

with *Yamada-san-o* instead of *onegai-shimasu* having the higher pitch. If you pronounce it the other way, as

Yamada-san-o ONEGAI-SHIMASU.

it will sound as if you are irritated or overbearing.

It is wrong to think that Japanese should be spoken in a monotone. The foreign speaker of Japanese should be aware that his tone conveys a message, which may be contrary to his intention. Thus an English-speaking person needs to be careful not to use an English tone in speaking Japanese, even though it is a difficult thing to do.

Doozo yoi otoshi-o

どうぞ　よい　お年を

(I wish you a happy new year)

When Mr. Lerner was leaving the office on the day before vacation started, he wanted to wish everybody at the office a happy new year. So just as people say "Merry Christmas" when parting even some days before Christmas, he said,

> *Shinnen omedetoo-gozaimasu.*
> (A Happy New Year!)

Everybody looked amazed and nobody answered him. Mr. Takada then told him that it was too early to use that greeting. He further explained that Japanese do not have the custom of saying *Omedetoo-gozaimasu* before the event. Instead of *Shinnen omedetoo-gozaimasu*, people say

> *Doozo yoi otoshi-o.*
> (*lit.* Please meet a good year.)

    *   *   *

Doozo yoi otoshi-o is the shortened form of *Doozo yoi otoshi-o omukae-kudasai.* This greeting is exchanged only when people are parting before the new year. This expression *yoi . . .o* is, however, limited to this greeting, and Japanese do not use this expression for other situations like wishing a good trip or a good weekend.

It is not that Japanese don't want to wish others good luck, but that there is no set expression for it.

50

When parting before the weekend, Japanese simply say *Sayoonara* or *Shitsuree-shimasu.* (Incidentally, *Sayoonara* or *Sayonara* does not sound polite and should not be used to a superior.)

To someone who has a cold or other minor illness

Doozo odaiji-ni.

(Please take good care of yourself.)

is used when parting.

To a person who is going on a long journey or leaving for a new job, such expressions are used as

Doozo oki-o tsukete.

(*lit.* Please be careful.)

Doozo ogenki-de.

(*lit.* Please be in good health.)

Between good friends, people sometimes say such things as "don't drink too much" or "do your best" or "hang in there."

The proper greeting to someone who is going out, either for work or pleasure, is

Itte-irasshai.

(*lit.* Please go and come back.)

There is no equivalent for the English, "Have a good time."

Some Japanese who are familiar with English expressions wish they could say similar things in Japanese, especially when they are asked by their foreign friends or acquaintances what they can say in Japanese. Some Japanese go ahead and say *Yoi shuumatsu-o* (Have a good weekend) or *Yoi go-ryokoo-o* (Have a good trip), but this still sounds like a direct translation from English. Only when parting at the end of the year can they say with peace of mind, as we also are happy to say,

Doozo yoi otoshi-o!
どうぞ　よい　お年を。

Akemashite omedetoo-gozaimasu

あけまして　おめでとうございます

(Happy New Year!)

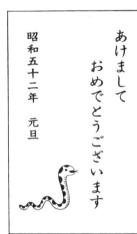

昭和五十二年　元旦

あけまして
おめでとうございます

On New Year's Day Mr. Lerner found dozens of greeting cards in his mailbox. Some of them had greetings in *kanji* and some in *hiragana*; some had a picture of a snake, the zodiac symbol for 1977. It was a very pleasant experience to see so many cards together, but he also wondered why they had all come on the same day. He remembered that he had not received a single New Year's card in December, while in the United States Christmas cards start coming early in December and gradually accumulate towards Christmas day.

*　　　*　　　*

New Year's cards mailed before a certain day in December (last month it was Dec. 20) will be delivered on New Year's Day. If you mail your cards later, they will be delivered any day either before or after New Year's Day, just as

52

regular mail is. Japanese try to mail their New Year's cards so that they can be delivered exactly on the Day because it is unseemly for them to arrive before the Day. This seems to be connected with the fact that the Japanese never exchange New Year's greetings before January the first.

New Year's greetings start with the New Year and usually continue to be exchanged for about two weeks.

The most common greetings corresponding to "Happy New Year" are the following two:

Shinnen omedetoo-gozaimasu.
(*lit.* We are happy to have the New Year.)

Akemashite omedetoo-gozaimasu.
(*lit.* We are happy that New Year's Day has dawned.)

And they are usually followed by

Sakunen-chuu-wa iroiro osewasama-ni narimashita.
Honnen-mo doozo yoroshiku onegai-itashi-masu.

These two sentences mean "Thank you very much for everything you did for me last year. Please continue to be kind to me."

We would now like to say to you,

Honnen-mo doozo yoroshiku onegai-itashi-masu.

本年も　どうぞ　よろしく　おねがいいたします。

Itadakimasu

いただきます

(I'm going to receive your treat.
Thank you)

A few days ago Mr. Takada asked Mr. Lerner to have dinner with his family. They had prepared the New Year's dinner, very colorful and very special. Mr. Lerner decided to be as polite as he could. So when Mr. Takada said according to Japanese custom

Nanimo gozaimasen-ga doozo (There isn't much but please start eating), Mr. Lerner said politely

Itadakimasu.
いただきます。

(Thank you. — *lit.* I'm going to receive your treat.)

Then everybody else said the same thing and started eating. Mr. Lerner was a little surprised because he had thought that *Itadakimasu* was used by a guest to thank his host.

*　　　*　　　*

Most people say *Itadakimasu* before eating and *Gochisoo-sama* after eating even in their own home. Children are trained at home never to forget to say these phrases, and when they go to kindergarten or elementary school teachers reinforce this training. Some people disregard this custom when they grow up, but others continue to say these phrases even when they eat alone.

Both *Itadakimasu* and *Gochisoosama* are expressions of gratitude. This gratitude is directed to everybody and everything that has made the meal possible. Thus they can be used both as an expression of gratitude to the host and as something like saying grace in the West.

When you are asked to start eating by your host, it is proper to say *Itadakimasu* before eating. And you should say *Gochisoosama* (*lit.* It was a real feast), or more politely, *Gochisoosama-deshita*, after eating. Then the host or hostess will say something to deny this praise, such as

Osomatsusama-deshita.
(You're welcome. —*lit.* It was a poor meal.)

It is not Japanese custom to say "I'm glad you liked it."

Another point about *Gochisoosama* is that it is used as an expression of thanks, not just for food, but also for hospitality. For instance, when leaving a party at someone's home, Americans might say to the host or hostess "Thank you very much. I had a wonderful time," but in Japan, people simply say

Gochisoosama-deshita.
ごちそうさまでした。

meaning "Thank you very much for everything you did to entertain me."

Shirimasen

知りません

(I don't know)

During the coffee break a few days ago Miss Yoshida asked Mr. Lerner if he had any plans for the next Saturday. Since he did not know yet, Mr. Lerner answered

Shirimasen.
知りません。
(I don't know.)

Miss Yoshida looked confused and asked Mr. Takada to help her. She said that she wanted to invite Mr. Lerner as well as Mr. Takada and a few others to a party at her home, but that she did not dare ask him because she didn't understand his answer.

What was wrong with saying *Shirimasen* for "I don't know?"

* * *

In the situation mentioned above, a Japanese would say

Wakarimasen.
わかりません。
(*lit.* I don't understand.)

instead of *Shirimasen.* In fact, Japanese say

Wakarimasen when English-speaking people would say "I don't know." When asked for directions or the time, Japanese often say *Wakarimasen* instead of *Shirimasen*.

Shirimasen means that "I haven't had the chance to get the information"; therefore it should be all right to say *Shirimasen* when you do not have the particular knowledge. But in actual usage Japanese prefer saying *Wakarimasen* when they think they should know the answer. Because one should know about oneself better than anything else, to say *Shirimasen* when asked what one is going to do in the future sounds very strange. It can be taken as a blunt statement meaning "It has nothing to do with me," as is actually used when one is angry. When an angry mother says *Shirimasen!* to her naughty child, it means she refuses to have anything to do with him for the time being.

Wakarimasen is preferred even when answering a question which does not directly concern oneself because it implies that the lack of knowledge is one's own fault. For example when a student cannot answer the instructor's question, he usually says *Wakarimasen*. It is more polite to say that he does not have the ability to find out than to say that he has not had the chance to learn; insisting on the latter may sound as if he is blaming his instructors for their negligence or is blaming the questioner for asking something he has not learned.

However, when the question is about something one is not expected to know, such as whether one knows a certain person or a place, it is all right to say *Shirimasen*. And also, when the question takes the form . . .-o *shitte-imasu-ka* or more politely, . . .-o *gozonji-desu-ka* (Do you know . . .?), the answer should be either *Hai, shitte-imasu,* or *Iie, shirimasen.*

Onegai-shimasu

おねがいします

(Excuse me)

The other day Mr. Lerner went into a little grocery store to buy some bread. It was deserted; the storekeeper seemed to be in the back watching TV. Mr. Lerner was wondering how he could get the storekeeper's attention when a Japanese woman came in and said,

> *Onegai-shimasu.*
> おねがいします。
> (Excuse me. — *lit.* Please do me a favor.)

After that Mr. Lerner observed the use of *onegai-shimasu* and found it to be a very convenient expression to know.

     *   *   *

There are several ways to attract a stranger's attention. You may hear *Chotto* or *Oi* being used but these are rather rude.

Moshimoshi is used not only to start a conversation on the telephone but also when addressing a stranger. When you have noticed that someone has dropped something, you may say

> *Moshimoshi, nanika ochimashita-yo.*
> (Excuse me, but you dropped something. —

lit. Something has dropped.)

When you need someone's help you can say *Onegai-shimasu* as well as *Sumimasen* or *Anoo*. *Onegai-shimasu* is used to call a clerk at a store or a waiter at a restaurant.

Onegai-shimasu is also used to mean "Please take care of this for me." When submitting papers such as application forms or bills in a government office, bank and the like, people say

Kore-o onegai-shimasu. (Please take care of this.) They do not usually use the particular verb such as to sign, to accept or to pay. *Onegai-shimasu* can stand for all these verbs.

Thus when concluding a business discussion one often says

Ja, yoroshiku onegai-shimasu.
(*lit.* Well then, please take care of it kindly.)

Yoroshiku onegai-shimasu
よろしく　おねがいします。

is also used when first meeting someone.

You may still remember hearing candidates saying over and over *Yoroshiku onegai-shimasu* during last year's general election. They seldom say directly "please vote for me"; *onegai-shimasu* is enough to convey their wishes and sounds more polite since it's not so direct.

Oneesan

おねえさん

(Older sister)

A few days ago Mr. Lerner had lunch with Miss Yoshida, and on their way back to the office, they dropped in at a little bookstore. A little boy there was absorbed in a comic book, blocking the narrow aisle so that Miss Yoshida could not go by. His mother noticed this and admonished him by saying,

Oneesan-no jama-ni narimasu-yo.
(You're standing in that lady's way. — *lit.* You're standing in your older sister's way.)

Mr. Lerner felt it strange that the mother called Miss Yoshida, a complete stranger, *oneesan* (older sister). But when he mentioned this to Miss Yoshida, she said it was perfectly all right and she was glad that she wasn't called *obasan* (aunt).

* * *

Family terms in Japanese are often used to address even those who are not family members.

Children always call strangers by family terms such as *oniisan* (older brother), *oneesan*, *ojisan* (uncle), *obasan* (aunt), *ojiisan* (grandfather), and *obaasan* (grandmother). Children use family terms when addressing someone they know, too. In fact, they never call older people by their names.

For instance, when a little boy thanks his friend's mother, he says, *Obasan, arigatoo* (Thank you — *lit.* Thank you, Aunt) and not *Takahashi-san, arigatoo* (Thank you, Mrs. Takahashi), which seems natural to a native English speaker. In fact, the latter will seem very strange to the Japanese ear.

When adults use family terms towards those who are not family members, it is customary to do so from a child's point of view. Thus, though Miss Yoshida is younger than the boy's mother, the mother called her *oneesan*. You have probably noticed people calling storekeepers and others *ojisan* or *obasan*.

おじさん or おばさん

This extended use of family terms, however, presupposes a certain degree of familiarity. Therefore it should be avoided when one wants to show respect rather than intimacy. *Ojisan* or *obasan* is not usually used towards doctors, teachers, lawyers, and others who are engaged in highly respected occupations; it is proper to call these people *sensee* (*lit.* teacher). Other people too, often dislike being called by family terms since it sounds too familiar. For instance, most girls working at restaurants and hotels do not like being called *oneesan*.

Itte-(i)rasshai

いって（い）らっしゃい

(Please go and come back)

One morning when Mr. Lerner was hurrying to the station, his neighbor Mrs. Okada who was sweeping the road in front of her house said,

Itte-(i)rasshai.
いって（い）らっしゃい。
(Have a nice day. — *lit.* Please go and come back.)

Mr. Lerner did not know how to respond to this greeting, so he just said *Sayoonara*, although he felt this was not quite right. Later at the office, Mr. Takada told him that he should have said

Itte-mairimasu or *Itte-kimasu.*
いってまいります　or　いってきます。
(Thank you, I will. — *lit.* I'll go and come back.)

*　　　*　　　*

Itte-(i)rasshai and *Itte-mairimasu* (or *Itte-kimasu*) are exchanged in a home when a family member leaves. It is customary for someone going out to say *Itte-mairimasu* or *Itte-kimasu* (less polite), and for those remaining to say *Itte-*

(i)rasshai.

Those expressions are also used between non-family members when they feel that they belong to the same group. The concept of "group" differs in its range depending on the individual, but usually people living in a neighborhood or people working at the same company are regarded as members of a group. Thus, these expressions are used when a neighbor or a member of a company leaves temporarily.

Sayoonara (Good-bye) is not used among family members unless they expect that they will not meet again. If a husband says to his wife *Sayoonara* when leaving, that means he is not going to live with her any more.

When a family member comes home, he says

Tadaima.
ただいま。
(I'm home. — *lit.* (I'm home) right now.)

And his family members say

Okaerinasai.
おかえりなさい。
(Welcome home. — *lit.* You have come home.)

In English, people use various expressions when leaving and coming home, but in Japan, set expressions are used for these occasions: such expressions as *Konnichiwa* (Good day), *Konbanwa* (Good evening) or *Sayoonara* are not used among family members.

Taihen-desu-ne

たいへんですね

(That's tough)

One Friday evening, Mr. Lerner had finished his work and was about to leave the office, but Mr. Takada was still working. He wanted to express his sympathy for Mr. Takada's having to work on Friday evening and was wondering what the appropriate expression would be when Miss Yoshida went by and said,

> *Taihen-desu-ne.*
> たいへんですね。
>
> (That's tough. — *lit.* It's terrible, isn't it?)

Mr. Takada smiled and said there wasn't much left to do and asked her not to worry.

A few days later, on a cold morning Mr. Lerner saw Mr. Okada, his neighbor, busy washing his car. He tried this expression *Taihen-desu-ne.* It produced a great effect. Mr. Okada smiled in a very friendly manner and said,

> *Raanaa-san-koso, samui-noni taihen-desu-ne.* (It's you, Mr. Lerner, that's having a terrible time when it's so cold.)

*   *   *

The word *taihen* means "unusual" or "terrible"; it can mean "an unusually hard job" or "a terrible experience." You can use this word to refer to your own condition or experience, for example,

Mainichi taihen-desu.
(I'm terribly busy every day.)

or

Kinoo-wa taihen-deshita.
(I had a terrible experience yesterday.)

The expression *Taihen-desu-ne* is often used in everyday conversation to show sympathy. You may have noticed that Japanese use this expression towards people working hard — businessmen working overtime, students studying hard to get into a good college, waitresses during the lunchtime rush, and so on.

The Japanese like to show respect for diligence even if a person may be working hard for his own personal benefit. They wish to build up good relations with others by expressing their appreciation of diligence and their sympathy for having to work hard.

Ocha-o doozo

お茶を　どうぞ

(Please have some tea)

The other day Mr. Lerner visited Mr. Takada. Mrs. Takada welcomed him and tried to make him comfortable, but she didn't say much. When Mr. Lerner later recalled what she had said, he realized that all her sentences had ended in *doozo*.

When he entered the *genkan*, or entrance, she said *Doozo*, meaning "Please come in." When she showed him into the room she offered him a *zabuton* to sit on, saying, *Doozo*. When she brought tea she said, *Ocha-o doozo*. She said *Moo sukoshi doozo* when she wanted him to have some more cookies. When he left, she said at the *genkan*, *Mata doozo*, meaning "Please come again." None of these sentences had included a verb.

*　　　*　　　*

Japanese tend to avoid saying what can be understood without mentioning it. In Mrs. Takada's sentences, the following verbs are understood.

どうぞ。

Doozo (*agatte-kudasai*, or *o-agari-kudasai*). — Please come in.

66

Doozo (*zabuton-o*) (*o-ate-kudasai*, or *o-shiki-kudasai*). — Please sit on the *zabuton*.

Ocha-o doozo (*nonde-kudasai*, or more politely, *meshiagatte-kudasai*). — Please have some tea.

Moo sukoshi doozo (*tabete-kudasai*, or more politely, *meshiagatte-kudasai*). — Please have some more.

また　どうぞ。

Mata doozo (*kite-kudasai*, or more politely, *oide-kudasai*). — Please come again.

In the above sentences, *doozo* can stand for the verb when the speaker's intention is clear. Sentences ending with just *doozo* show a reserved attitude and therefore sound more polite to the Japanese ear.

You will notice that when the Japanese use sentences with *doozo*, they make their intentions clear by bowing or using other gestures.

Ojama-shimasu

おじゃまします

(I'm going to bother you)

A reporter came to see Mr. Lerner at his office last week to interview him about his life as a foreigner working in Japan. When she came into his office she said,

Ojama-shimasu.
おじゃまします。
(May I interrupt you? — *lit.* I'm going to bother you.)

When she left, she bowed and said,

Ojama-shimashita.
おじゃましました。
(I'm sorry I took your time. — *lit.* I've bothered you.)

*　　*　　*

The verb *ojama-suru* means "to bother" or "to be in someone's way" and it is used in practice to refer to talking to, or visiting, a person either at home or at work.

Ojama-shimasu is used when one starts talking and *Ojama-shimashita* is used when one has finished talking and leaves. *Ojama-shimasu* is often preceded by *chotto*, and *ojama-shimashita* by *doomo*. Thus:

> *Chotto ojama-shimasu.*
> (May I interrupt you for a moment?)
> *Doomo ojama-shimashita.*
> (I'm very sorry I took your time.)

Similar expressions are *Shitsuree-shimasu* (*lit.* I'm going to be rude) and *Shitsuree-shimashita* (*lit.* I have been rude). The former is used when starting a conversation and the latter when concluding it, and *chotto* and *doomo* are added to them just as they are to *ojama-shimasu* and *ojama-shimashita*.

However, *shitsuree* can be used to refer to various actions besides talking; also *shitsuree-shimasu* is often used when one leaves as well as arrives because *shitsuree*, "a rude action," can refer to the action of leaving. Thus it is possible to say

> *Doomo shitsuree-shimashita. Dewa kore-de shitsuree-shimasu.*
> (I'm very sorry I took your time. Now please excuse me.)

On the other hand, *ojama shimasu* is used only when starting a conversation and not when leaving. If you say *Ojama-shimasu* when you are leaving, the listener will be quite puzzled.

Moo kaeranakucha

もう　かえらなくちゃ

(I must go home now)

A few weeks ago several people gathered at Mr. Lerner's house and had a pleasant evening together. At about 9 Miss Yoshida said,

Moo kaeranakucha.
もう　かえらなくちゃ。
(*lit.* If I don't go home now.)

Mr. Lerner didn't clearly understand but guessed that she meant that she had to go home then.

After that Mr. Lerner paid attention to how Japanese finish their sentences and found that often they end like Miss Yoshida's sentence, namely just giving the condition and omitting the conclusion.

*　　　*　　　*

After *kaeranakucha* (a contraction of *kaeranakute-wa*) *narimasen* (it won't do) or a phrase meaning "my family will be worried" or the like is understood. Thus *Moo kaeranakucha* alone can be translated as "I must go home now."

When the situation permits, Japanese tend to use incomplete sentences. In fact, they feel it is rather clumsy to say the whole thing when mentioning the first half suffices. Thus, to indicate that they want to leave soon, the Japanese will often say just *Sorosoro* (*lit.* slowly; abbreviation of *Sorosoro oitoma-itashimasu*, meaning "Soon I'll leave") or *Jaa, kore-de* (*lit.* Well, with this or Well, at this point).

Nowadays students studying for exams keep telling themselves *Ganbaranakucha* (*lit.* If I don't keep at it). The meaning is obvious; if they don't work hard, they will fail in their exams so they have to work hard. In a similar way, we often tell ourselves

Ganbaranakucha.
がんばらなくちゃ。

because if we don't try hard, you will stop reading this column.

Okagesama-de

おかげさまで

(Thanks to you)

The other day Mr. Lerner helped Mr. Takada with his work after finishing his own. Mr. Takada thanked him by saying,

Okagesama-de hayaku sumimashita.
(I finished quickly thanks to your help.)

A few days later, when Mr. Lerner asked Mr. Okada, his neighbor, if his son had passed the college entrance exam, he answered,

Hai, okagesama-de.
はい、おかげさまで。
(Yes, thank you. — *lit.* Yes, thanks to you.)

Mr. Lerner felt it strange to be thanked when he had not done anything to help Mr. Okada's son.

*　　*　　*

Okagesama-de is used to express gratitude either to a particular person or to all that has been helpful.

A grateful patient will say to his doctor

Okagesama-de yoku narimashita.
(Thanks to you, I've recovered.)

72

And also when an acquaintance asks how he feels, he will say,

Okagesama-de yoku narimashita.

He doesn't mean that the acquaintance has helped him recover from the illness; he means that he feels grateful for all the factors that have made his recovery possible, including the acquaintance.

This expression *Okagesama-de* is sometimes used simply as a formality in such exchanges as

A: *Ogenki-desu-ka.* (How are you? — *lit.* Are you well?)
B: *Okagesama-de.* (Fine, thank you.)
and
A: *Oshigoto-wa doo-desu-ka.* (How's your work?)
B: *Okagesama-de.* (Thank you. It's going well.)

However, there always is the underlying idea that one should be grateful to what has been of help, even without one's knowledge. Even if one's success obviously comes from one's own effort, it is regarded as good to attribute it to others; this is why Mr. Okada said *Okagesama-de* to Mr. Lerner when he informed that his son has passed the entrance exam.

Kochira-koso

こちらこそ

(I should say that)

Mr. Lerner and Mr. Takada had completed some business with Mr. Saito and were leaving, when Mr. Saito said *Doomo shitsuree-shimashita* (*lit.* I have been rude to you) to thank them. In reply, Mr. Lerner said *Doo-itashimashite* (Not at all), but Mr. Takada said

Kochira-koso.
こちらこそ。
(*I* should say that. — *lit.* It is my side.)

This expression was new to Mr. Lerner and he wondered how it compared with *Doo-itashimashite*, but Mr. Takada seemed busy so he didn't ask him.

*   *   *

Kochira-koso literally means "It's this side," or "It's my side." It is actually used to mean that the speaker is to blame rather than the person who has apologized.

In reply to an apology both *Kochira-koso* and *Doo-itashimashite* can be used, but there is some difference between the two. For example, when someone says to you

Shitsuree-shimashita.

saying *Doo-itashimashite* denies the other person's being rude to you while saying *Kochira-koso* indicates that you are blaming yourself for being rude. Therefore *Kochira-koso* is more appropriate when both you and the other person are involved in the matter.

When someone meets you after a long time and says

Gobusata-itashimashita (I'm sorry I didn't write to you — or, call on you — for a long time), you should not say *Doo-itashimashite*, because it implies that the lack of communication was solely his fault and further, that you are not very interested in communicating with him. It is therefore much better to say *Kochira-koso*.

Kochira-koso is used most often when two people meet for the first time.

A: *Hajimemashite. Doozo yoroshiku.*
　　はじめまして。どうぞ　よろしく。

(How do you do? Glad to meet you. — *lit.* This is the first time. Please be kind to me.)

B: *Kochira-koso (doozo yoroshiku).*

(The pleasure is mine.)

Shujin-ga osewa-ni natte-orimasu

主人が　おせわに　なっております

(Thank you for taking care of my husband)

When Mr. Lerner was introduced to Mrs. Takada, the wife of his co-worker, she said,

Shujin-ga itsumo osewa-ni natte-orimasu.
主人が　いつも　おせわに　なっております。
(*lit.* My husband is always taken care of by you.)

Mr. Lerner did not exactly understand what she had said, but guessed that she was thanking him for something he had done for her husband, and simply said *Iie* in reply.

(Later he learned that *Iie* was all right but that *Kochira-koso* is the most appropriate answer.)

*　　*　　*

Osewa-ni naru literally means "to be taken care of." *Shujin-ga osewa-ni natte-orimasu* sounds strange if translated literally, but this expression is actually used to mean "Thank you for your kindnesses to my husband."

It is customary to use this expression when introduced to an acquaintance of one's family members. Just as a wife says *Shujin-ga . . .* a husband says *Kanai-ga* (My wife) *. . .* and par-

76

ents say *Kodomo-ga* (My child) . . . (or they mention the name of their child such as *Kazuo-ga* . . .) Parents use this expression without fail towards their child's teacher or doctor.

As is true with other expressions, this expression too can be used simply as a formality. A wife may say *Shujin-ga osewa-ni natte-orimasu* when she is really grateful as well as when she feels that the listener does not particularly deserve her gratitude.

We can see two important underlying ideas behind this expression. One is that the Japanese feel it essential to express their gratitude for favors done for their family members just as if they had received them themselves. Another idea is that the state of being associated with someone should be regarded as *osewa-ni naru* because one may be receiving favors from him even if one doesn't realize it at the time.

Anoo . . .

あのう……

(Excuse me . . .)

One afternoon a young woman came to see Mr. Takada about some business. Mr. Lerner was in the same room and observed how they talked. The woman started by saying,

Anoo . . .
(Well, . . .)

and waiting for Mr. Takada to say *Hai*, before getting down to business. She often said *Anoo* before starting a new sentence during their discussion, too.

Mr. Lerner had heard that *anoo* was the Japanese equivalent of the English "er . . . ," which one uses when looking for the right word, so he thought that its frequent use indicated poor language ability. But when he remarked later that the woman was a poor speaker, Mr. Takada did not agree. In fact he said that he liked the way she spoke because it sounded modest.

*   *   *

Anoo is sometimes used merely as a stopgap phrase when one cannot think of the right word; in this usage it resembles the English "er . . ." But *anoo* is very often used consciously and intentionally for other purposes altogether.

Anoo indicates that the speaker is not yet ready to speak up; it is used to show his hesitation. To sound hesitant or reserved (needless to say, one also acts reserved at the same time) is appropriate in certain situations. For example, when speaking to a superior, one should not sound too ready to speak up; he should express his awe or reserve. Also one should sound hesitant when making a request. In this case *Anoo* is often followed by other expressions such as *sumimasen-ga* or *osoreirimasu-ga*.

Anoo also is used by itself as a signal to start a conversation so that when someone says *Anoo. . .* in a reserved way, the listener usually answers

Hai, or *Hai, nan-deshoo-ka* (Yes, what can I do for you?)

without waiting for the speaker to continue. Thus *Anoo. . .* is used to mean "Excuse me, but may I speak to you?"

Ano-ne is a little different from *Anoo*. Although it also functions as a signal to show that one is going to speak, it indicates intimacy rather than politeness. *Ano-ne* cannot be used towards one's superiors; it can only be used in familiar speech.

79

Jitsu-wa . . .

じつは……

(Well, . . .)

One evening Mr. Lerner was visited by his neighbor, Mr. Okada. Mr. Okada commented on the weather being changeable, talked about how every one of his family had caught bad colds, and then complained about things getting more expensive every month. He seemed prepared to go on this way forever, and Mr. Lerner started wondering how he could ask him what his business was in a polite way in Japanese. Finally Mr. Okada said,

Jitsu-wa . . .
じつは……
(In fact, . . .)

and got down to business. The business was concluded quite quickly. In fact, Mr. Okada had spent much more time on the preceding talk.

*　　　*　　　*

Jitsu-wa literally means "in fact" or "as a matter of fact," but in actual practice it is used to indicate that one is going to start discussing business. It actually means "I'm going to discuss business now," "I'm going to make a request," and the like.

80

(*Jitsu-ni* means "indeed" or "really," and is used for emphasis. For example, *Jitsu-ni omo-shiroi-desu-ne* means "It's really interesting." *Jitsu-wa* and *Jitsu-ni* must be carefully distinguished.)

Some people might think that what is said before *Jitsu-wa* has no substantial meaning. This is true in a sense, but these preliminaries actually serve an important purpose in communication.

Most Japanese feel it necessary to spend considerable time and energy in building good relations with someone before discussing business with him. These good relations can be formed by confirming that the two people feel the same way about something. The subject matter must be chosen from this viewpoint; therefore, weather, one's family and the cost of living are usually good topics.

Jitsu-wa is a signal for starting business just as *Anoo* is a signal for starting a conversation. Thus:

Anoo . . . jitsu-wa . . . chotto onegai-ga aru-n-desuga. . .

あのう… じつは… ちょっと お願いが
あるんですが……

(Excuse me, but could I ask you to do a favor for me?)

Ichioo oazukari-shimasu

いちおう　おあずかりします

(I'll keep it for the time being)

The other day Mr. Lerner met Mr. Saito, an acquaintance, on the street, and they had dinner together at a restaurant. When they finished eating, Mr. Saito quickly took the bill and paid for both of them, but Mr. Lerner insisted on paying half. After refusing a couple of times, Mr. Saito accepted the money saying,

> *Ja, ichioo oazukari-shimasu.*
> じゃ、いちおう　おあずかりします。
> (Then I'll keep it for the time being.)

Mr. Lerner thought that Mr. Saito would return the money later, but when he met him the next time, he never mentioned it. Then Mr. Lerner checked the words *ichioo* and *azukaru* in the dictionary but he could not exactly understand how they are actually used.

＊　　　＊　　　＊

According to the dictionary, *ichioo* means "once" or "for the time being," and *azukaru* means "to keep for someone" or "to be entrusted with something"; thus, *Ichioo oazukari-shimasu* literally means "I'll keep it for the time being," and it was natural that Mr. Lerner thought that

82

the money would be returned.

But in actual practice, *ichioo* is used to imply that there is little chance that the speaker's intention can be realized. When one says *Ichioo oazukari-shimasu*, he means that although he will try to return it some time in the future, he may not be able to do so.

Because of this implication *ichioo* is very often used to politely refuse a request. If you ask someone to do you a favor and he says

Ichioo yatte-mimashoo.
いちおう　やってみましょう。
(I'll try.),

he means that he will try but he doubts if he can do it. It can be either that he is not willing to do it, or that he's willing to try but he's not confident in his own ability, or it can be that he's so modest that he doesn't want to promise you that he will be able to do it.

What the speaker really means when he says *Ichioo yatte-mimashoo* can be judged to some extent by his personality or the situation. But this judgment is sometimes difficult so one must be careful; a misunderstanding can result if you take this expression literally, especially when making a request that involves public services or bureaucratic procedures.

Ah, soo-ka, . . .soo-desu-ka

ああ、そうか……そうですか

(Oh, I see, . . .is that so?)

One afternoon Mr. Lerner was explaining a plan to Mr. Okada. The plan was rather complicated so it took some time for Mr. Okada to understand. When he finally understood it, he said,

Ah, soo-ka, . . .soo-desu-ka.
ああ、そうか……そうですか。
(Oh, I see, . . .is that so?)

Mr. Lerner wondered why he had said the same thing twice in different levels of speech (*soo-ka* is the plain equivalent of *soo-desu-ka*); Mr. Lerner's Japanese teacher had always corrected him when he mixed familiar with polite speech.

* * *

Mr. Okada had been speaking politely, ending his sentences with *-masu* and *-desu*. When he suddenly said *Soo-ka*, he was talking to himself; he was thinking aloud for a moment and immediately returned to normal speech when he said *Soo-desu-ka* to Mr. Lerner.

This type of shift is made in a conversation between two people who are not close enough to talk in familiar speech all the time but do not have to be strictly polite. Using the familiar level for a moment has the effect of adding intimacy; it is like letting down one's hair for a moment to reveal an aspect that one does not normally show.

And this is usually done when one is absorbed (or when one wants to appear absorbed) in the conversation. Mr. Okada, by saying *Soo-ka*, showed that Mr. Lerner's explanation was so good that he could understand the matter perfectly and he was very happy about it. The idea is that the speaker is so interested in the conversation that he can't be bothered to pay attention to politeness. This is why people in the midst of polite speech will often say *Ah, soo-ka,*

Ah, soo-yuu wake-ka.
ああ、そういう　わけか。
(Oh, so that's it.)
Naruhodo-nee.
なるほどねえ。
(Oh, I see.)

When making this shift, the less polite expression must be said with a completely different tone; either it should sharply fall towards the end or in a much lower voice. It is important that you sound deeply impressed; if you say it with the same tone as the rest of the conversation, it will sound abrupt and rude.

This shift is sometimes made on purpose in public speaking too as an effective way to win the audience by revealing what the speaker does not usually show in public.

Nikkoo-e ikitai-desu

日光へ　いきたいです

(I want to go to Nikko)

Mr. Lerner's sister Margaret wrote that she was coming to Japan next month. Mr. Takada and Miss Yoshida, his co-workers, started discussing which of various famous spots he should take her to first. Mr. Lerner recalled what Margaret had said in her letter and said,

Nikkoo-e ikitai-desu.

meaning "she wants to go to Nikko."

But Miss Yoshida said, *Ara, Raanaa-san-mo?* (Oh, you too, Mr. Lerner?), obviously taking his comment as "I want to go to Nikko." Mr. Lerner had been told by his Japanese teacher that one does not have to mention the subject of the sentence unless it has to be emphasized. Did he have to start his sentence with *Imooto-wa . . .* (My sister . . .)?

*　　*　　*

Miss Yoshida would not have misunderstood Mr. Lerner if he had said

Nikkoo-e ikitagatte-imasu.
日光へ　いきたがっています。
(She wants to go to Nikko),

instead of saying *Nikkoo-e ikitai-desu*. Words ending in *-tai* are used to indicate the speaker's wishes while those ending in *-tagaru* are used to show the wishes of someone else. Thus *ikitai-desu* usually means "I want to go," and *ikita-gatte-imasu* means "he wants to go," "she wants to go," or "they want to go."

In a similar way, certain expressions that are used to express the speaker's feelings cannot be used for third persons. For instance, *Ureshii-desu* or *Kanashii-desu* means "I'm happy." or "I'm unhappy." It is not appropriate to say *Yoshida-san-wa ureshii-desu* (Miss Yoshida is happy) or *Imooto-wa kanashii-desu* (My sister is unhappy). When referring to others, you have to change the last part of the words:

> *Yoshida-san-wa ureshisoo-desu.*
> (Miss Yoshida looks happy.)
> *Imooto-wa kanashisoo-desu.*
> (My sister looks unhappy.)

The idea behind this distinction is that one cannot know another's feelings with certainty but can only judge by his appearance. In other words, you cannot say that someone is happy in Japanese; you must say he looks happy.

Returning to the distinction between *ikitai* and *ikitagaru*, the same logic can be seen; only the speaker himself knows what he wants to do, and in referring to others one has to use *-tagaru* which means "to act like wanting to do some-thing."

This distinction between expressions refer-ring to the speaker himself and those referring to others is one of the devices that makes it possible to often omit the subject of the sentence in Japa-nese.

Yomoo-to omoimasu

よもうと　おもいます

(I think I'll read them)

A few days ago Mr. Lerner decided to take home some of the papers he could not finish reading during the day, and was putting them together when Mr. Takada came to see if he was ready to leave. So Mr. Lerner said, pointing to the papers,

Konban yomu-to omoimasu.

meaning "I think I'll read them tonight." But Mr. Takada did not understand and asked *Darega?* (Who's going to?) Mr. Lerner wondered why he asked this; several people had told him that one does not have to mention the subject of the sentence in Japanese when it can be understood from the context.

* * *

If Mr. Lerner had said

Konban yomoo-to omoimasu.
こんばん　よもうと　おもいます。

instead of *Konban yomu-to omoimasu*, Mr. Takada would have immediately understood.

Saying *Yomu-to omoimasu* means that the

speaker thinks someone else will read them, instead of the speaker reading them himself.

To indicate the speaker's own intention, a different form of the verb must be used before . . . *to omoimasu* (I think . . .). This form is usually called the volitional; *yomoo* is the volitional form of *yomu*, and *ikoo* (I'll go) is that of *iku* (to go).

Japanese leave out the subject of the sentence whenever they can, but there are certain devices or rules to avoid confusion or misunderstanding. The use of the various verb forms is one of those devices. *Yomoo-to omoimasu* and *Yomu-to omoimasu* are as completely different sentences as "I think I'll read them" and "I think he'll read them" in English.

If asked what you will do tomorrow and you answer

Tsuri-ni iku-to omoimasu.,

meaning that you intend to go fishing, the listener will be a little puzzled. Although it is clear from the situation that you are referring to yourself, it will still seem strange because it sounds as if you were talking about someone else.

You must be especially careful when you want to add that you don't know for sure yet. If you say

Tsuri-ni iku-to omoimasu-ga, yoku shirimasen.,

it is even more puzzling because it definitely means that you are talking about someone else. Instead you should say

Tsuri-ni ikoo-ka-to omoimasu-ga, mada yoku wakarimasen.

(I think I might go fishing, but I don't know for sure yet — the *ka* added to *ikoo* shows uncertainty.)

Yappari . . .

やっぱり……

(After all . . .)

A few days ago while walking down the street, Mr. Lerner suddenly realized that he was lost. So he called to a young man passing by and asked him how to get to the nearest subway station. The young man said,

Soo-desu-nee . . . Yappari kono michi-o massugu itte. . .

そうですねえ……やっぱり　この　道を　まっすぐ
いって……

(*lit*. That's right. After all, you go straight along this street and . . .)

Mr. Lerner had learned that the first phrase *Soo-desu-nee* actually means "Well, let me see," but he did not understand why the young man had used *yappari*. According to the dictionary, *yappari* means "after all," or "as I expected;" but the young man had not said anything before that.

This usage is not limited to this young man. Mr. Lerner had heard a lot of Japanese start their sentences with *yappari*, especially when replying to a question.

*　　*　　*

The word *yappari* seems to be used so often

with no particular meaning that even some Japanese say it has no meaning and its usage should be avoided. But this word is meaningful in communication.

When the young man said to Mr. Lerner *Yappari kono michi-o itte . . .*, this *yappari* is used to mean "I have thought about many possible ways to get to the nearest station and *after all* I think it is best to go this way." In a sense, it shows that the speaker is answering the question conscientiously. This is why Japanese often start their replies with *yappari.*

The effect produced by this use of *yappari* depends on the situation. It is appropriate and friendly when one is answering a question to help another. But when one starts with this word in giving one's opinion without being asked, it gives the impression of being overly self-assertive or even aggressive.

It also gives the impression that the topic has already been discussed between the speaker and the listener, thus producing an air of intimacy. Some people purposely take advantage of this effect; for example, a salesman will resort to this word when trying to persuade a potential buyer:

Yappari kore-ga ichiban-desu-yo
(After all this is the best)

even when he is not actually making any comparison.

Yappari is one of those words that is used in informal speech where one can express his emotions more freely; in formal speech, the word *kekkyoku* is used to mean "after all" because it sounds less emotional.

Burabura shite-imashita

ぶらぶら　していました

(I was loafing around)

One Monday morning Miss Yoshida asked Mr. Lerner what he had done over the weekend. Mr. Lerner tried using a new expression:

Uchi-de furafura shite-imashita.

meaning "I was home, just loafing around." Miss Yoshida looked concerned and asked if he was all right. She even suggested leaving early and going to see a doctor.

What Mr. Lerner said actually meant "I was weak and felt dizzy." He should have said,

Uchi-de burabura shite-imashita.
うちで　ぶらぶら　していました。

*　　　*　　　*

Some words are made from imitating sounds; these words are called onomatopoeia. In English there are such onomatopoetic words as "bow-wow," "cuckoo," "chitchat," "bang," and so on. In Japanese there are numerous words of this kind, such as *furafura*, *burabura*, and *sorosoro* (slowly). These words are used quite often in conversation, and further, some of them are even used in literary works by noted authors.

These words can be very effective when used correctly or skillfully, but in order to use them correctly, it is necessary to understand what impression some sounds give. For instance, the *ko* sound is used to describe something small and light while the *go* sound stands for something big and heavy; *korokoro* describes the rolling of something small like a baseball or pencil, while *gorogoro* describes the rolling of something heavy like a log. An office worker might say, in telling how he spent his holiday,

Uchi-de gorogoro shite-imashita.

to mean that he was stretching and moving around lazily perhaps in front of the TV set.

Fu and *bu* are also in contrast. Thus when someone is in the state described as *furafura*, he is weak and unsteady from fatigue, sickness, or excessive drinking. *Burabura* shows an aimless motion, but does not imply the fragility that *furafura* does.

Similarly, *zo* sounds stronger and often unpleasant compared with *so*. People say cockroaches move *zorozoro* (in herds); if you say *sorosoro*, it sounds as if the cockroaches are moving about quietly and in a considerate manner.

Ocha-demo nomimasen-ka

お茶でも　のみませんか

(How about having some tea?)

A few days ago Mr. Lerner ran into Mr. Okada on the street. Mr. Okada suggested that they go to a coffee shop nearby, saying

Ocha-demo nomimasen-ka.
お茶でも　のみませんか。
(How about having some tea?)

At the coffee shop, however, he actually ordered coffee instead of tea, and Mr. Lerner learned that *demo* in *ocha-demo* means ". . . or something like that" rather than "even."

Then yesterday afternoon, when Miss Yoshida asked what his sister Margaret was studying in college, he was not sure so he said

Suugaku-demo benkyoo-shite-imasu.

meaning "She's studying mathematics or something like that." Miss Yoshida understood but said that *suugaku-demo* somehow sounded strange.

*　　　*　　　*

Demo meaning ". . . or something like that" is quite often used when suggesting, as in

94

Eega-demo mimashoo-ka.
(How about going to a movie?)
Satoo-san-demo sasoimashoo.
(Let's ask Mr. Sato.)

In such situations, *ocha-demo* or *eega-demo* is preferred to *ocha-o* or *eega-o* because it lets the listener choose what he likes among several possibilities. You can order coffee or coke instead of tea at a coffee shop when you have said *ocha-demo* instead of *ocha-o*.

Demo is also used when offering advice:

A: *Mada jikan-ga aru-n-desu-kedo.* (I have some time to kill.)
B: *Ja, shinbun-demo yondara doo-desu-ka.* (Then why don't you read a newspaper or something?)

But *demo* in this sense cannot be used to state a fact or to refer to what actually happened. Therefore *Suugaku-demo benkyoo-shite-imasu* cannot be accepted. Mr. Lerner should have said, *Suugaku-ka nanika benkyoo-shite-imasu* to mean "She's studying mathematics or something like that." *Ka nanika* can be used both in suggesting something and in stating a fact.

Thus:

Hima-dattara shinbun-demo yondara doo-desu-ka. Asoko-ni Japan Taimuzu-ka nanika ari-masu-yo.

(If you have some time to kill, why don't you read a newspaper? There's a Japan Times or something over there.)

Chotto. . .

ちょっと……

(A little bit. . .)

A few weeks ago Mr. Lerner and Miss Yoshida were having coffee during their break at work, when Mr. Takada came and asked them if they could come to his house on the next Saturday. Mr. Lerner said he would come, but Miss Yoshida said,

Sono hi-wa chotto. . .
その 日は ちょっと……
(*lit.* That day is a little bit. . .)

Then Mr. Takada immediately said he hoped she could come next time, without waiting for her to complete the sentence. Later he explained to Mr. Lerner that *chotto* stood for *chotto tsugoo-ga warui-n-desu* (it's little bit inconvenient for me).

But yesterday afternoon Miss Yoshida came to Mr. Lerner and said,

Anoo, chotto. . .
あのう、ちょっと……
(*lit.* Excuse me, a little bit. . .)

It took some time for him to understand that she meant *Chotto onegai-ga aru-n-desu-ga* (Will you do a little favor for me?).

*　　*　　*

Chotto is used in several different ways in daily conversation. It is used most often in requests and refusals.

When making a request, *chotto* is used to start the sentence as in

Chotto matte-kudasai.
 (Please wait a moment.)
Chotto onegai-shimasu.
(Please do me a favor.)

In such sentences *chotto* can be left out, but when it is included, it shows the speaker's reluctance to trouble others so that the sentences sound more reserved and considerate. In doing this, however, it must be said with a hesitant tone and is often preceded by *Anoo* or *Ano.* If *Chotto!* alone is said without a hesitant tone, it sounds rude. (Some people use it when calling to someone they do not know on the street, but it is impolite.)

When refusing, *chotto* is very convenient because it shows the speaker's reluctance. If someone answers your request with

Sore-wa chotto. . .
それは　ちょっと……

he means that he cannot do it but is unhappy to tell you so.

Reluctance is also appropriate when giving a negative evaluation. If you show your plan to someone and he says,

Chotto. . .
ちょっと……

It means he has some reservations about it. He can be more specific by saying

Koko-ga chotto. . .
(*lit.* In this point a little bit. . .)
or
Hiyoo-no ten-de chotto. . .
(*lit.* In terms of cost, a little bit. . .)

From Mr. Lerner's Diary

Mr. Lerner's diary mostly concerns usage of Japanese and might be called Nihongo Diary. With his permission, we'd like to show you some excerpts from it.

*   *   *

April 18
Mr. Okada came to the office to see me this afternoon. When he left, I said according to Japanese custom, *Waza-to oide-kudasatte doomo. . .*, meaning "Thank you very much for coming to see me." Mr. Okada answered politely as he always does; but Miss Yoshida, who happened to be with us, burst out laughing.

She said that what I had said reminded her of the drunkard who sat next to her on the train last night. The man *waza-to yorikakatte-kita* (purposely leaned against her). Now I know the difference between the two words. Thank you, Miss Yoshida.

> **wazawaza** (go to the trouble of . . .)
>   わざわざ
as in *Wazawaza oide-kudasatte doomo. . .*
>   **waza-to** (intentionally)
>   わざと
as in *Waza-to yorikakatte-kita.*

*   *   *

May 17
After listening to me talk for a while, *Sensee* (Mr. Lerner calls his Japanese teacher this way) reminded me that *to* meaning "and" is used only to connect nouns or pronouns, not to connect phrases or sentences.

It is correct to say:

Tanaka-san-to okusan-ni aimashita.
(I met Mr. Tanaka and his wife.)
or:
Ocha-to okashi-o kaimashita.
お茶と　おかしを　かいました。
(I bought some tea and cakes.)

But it is wrong to say
　— *Tanaka-san-ni aimashita-to iroiro hana-shimashita.* (I met Mr. Tanaka and talked about various things.)
　— *Ocha-o nomimashita-to okashi-o tabema-shita.* (I drank some tea and ate some cakes.)
I should say instead:

Tanaka-san-ni atte iroiro hanashimashita.
or:
Ocha-o nondari okashi-o tabetari shimashita.

*　　　*　　　*

June 7

I put my foot in my mouth again today. When I introduced Miss Winters to my Japanese friends I meant to say *Edo-bungaku-o kenkyuu-shite-imasu* (She's studying the literature of the Edo period). But my "d" sounded like an "r," so what I actually said was "She's studying pornographic literature." I don't want to think about how my friends laughed and Miss Winters blushed. I hate Japanese!

I then remembered what *Sensee* told me about the pronunciation of the "d" sound; I should have pressed the tip of the tongue against the upper teeth ridge. I will practice saying such words as *mado* (window), *kado* (corner) and so forth after recovering from today's shock. I resolve to say *Edo* 100 times tomorrow!

江戸文学　vs.　エロ文学

99

Atsuku natta-n-desu-ne

あつく　なったんですね

(It has gotten hot, hasn't it?)

Mr. Lerner has been paying attention lately to how Japanese end their sentences and finds that they use *n-desu* at the end as much as *masu* and *desu*; in other words, they often say *Itta-n-desu* (I went) rather than *Ikimashita* and *Isogashii-n-desu* (I'm busy) rather than *Isogashii-desu*.

Yesterday morning he used this form and said to Mr. Takada,

Atsuku natta-n-desu-ne.

meaning "It has gotten hot, hasn't it?"

Mr. Takada hesitated for a moment before he said *Soo-desu-ne*. It was as if he was trying to find out what Mr. Lerner really meant.

After this, Mr. Lerner carefully listened to people talking about the weather, and found that they always say

Atsuku narimashita-ne.

あつく　なりましたね。

or

Kinoo-wa yoku furimashita-ne.

(It rained a lot yesterday),

but they never say *Atsuku natta-n-desu-ne* or *Kinoo-wa yoku futta-n-desu-ne* when they open a conversation by referring to the weather.

*   *   *

While *Atsuku narimashita-ne* simply states a fact, *Atsuku natta-n-desu-ne* presupposes a certain situation. The implication can vary; it can be that the speaker has noticed that someone, including the listener, has changed into summer clothes; it can be that someone looks tired from the heat or is having a cold drink. In other words, *Atsuku natta-n-desu-ne* can be paraphrased as "It's because it has gotten hot."

Sentences ending in *n-desu-ka* are not used in asking questions to start a conversation either unless there is a certain situation. For example, if you say to someone

Isogashii-desu-ka. (Are you busy?),

you are simply asking whether he is busy or not. But if you say

Isogashii-n-desu-ka.

it can mean "Do you look tired because you are so busy?" "Are you so busy that you can't come with us to have a drink?" and so forth depending on the situation. Thus questions ending in *n-desu-ka* can imply various emotions such as concern, surprise, irritation, and criticism. If you ask them without the appropriate situation, the listener will be puzzled or even insulted.

From Mr. Lerner's Diary

April 1

Mr. Okada said today he was looking for a new secretary. When I asked what had happened to Miss Aoyama, I thought he said that she had died. I was surprised at the casual way that he announced the death of a beautiful young woman. Since it was April 1st, I asked him if he was putting me on. He said, *Iie, kekkon-suru-node yameta-n-desu.* (No, she quit because she's going to get married.)

Just before starting to say something, I realized that I hadn't heard the first sound of his sentence *Inaku narimashita* (She left us), and took it to be *Nakunarimashita* (She passed away).

いなく　なりました　vs.　なくなりました

*　　　*　　　*

May 13

When I arrived at the office this morning, Miss Yoshida called to say that she would be about an hour late. When Mr. Takada wondered if she was coming, I said *Ee, kite-imasu-yo.* He immediately left but came back after 5 minutes and said angrily, *Inai-ja arimasen-ka.* (She isn't here!) I said, *Ee, juuji-goro kite-imasu-yo.* Mr. Takada shrugged his shoulders as he always does when I have made a mistake in Japanese.

> To mean "someone is coming" I should say: *Kimasu.*　きます
> To mean "someone has come" I should say: *Kite-imasu.*　きています

*　　　*　　　*

June 10

I made Miss Yoshida laugh again! She

showed me a couple of picture books she had bought for her niece. They were fairy tales that I had read when I was very young, so I said

Watashi-mo wakai toki-ni yomimashita.
(I read them when I was young.)

Miss Yoshida said *E?* (What?), so I added,
Iie, haha-ga yonde-kuremashita.
(No, my mother read them to me.)

After laughing a long time, she said that my sentence made her think of a young man 17 to 25 years old sitting close to his mother and listening to her read picture books to him! It was all because of my misuse of the word *wakai*.

Wakai hito refers to people older than 16 or so. わかい　ひと

I should have said *chiisai toki* or *kodomo-no toki*. ちいさい　とき　or　こどもの　とき

Sumimasen

すみません

(I'm sorry)

Mr. Lerner was invited to dinner by the Takadas last Saturday. He took some candy with him for the Takada's little son. When he handed it to the boy Mrs. Takada said

Maa, doomo sumimasen. (*lit.* Oh, I'm very sorry), and urged her son to thank him. The little boy said

Ojisan, arigatoo. (Thank you, Mr. Lerner — *lit.* Thank you, uncle), and then added *gozaimasu* to make his expression more polite; perhaps he remembered that he had always been told to be polite.

When Mr. Lerner started learning Japanese, he thought that *Sumimasen* just meant "I'm sorry" or "Excuse me," and wondered why Japanese apologize when they should thank. Now he knows that *Sumimasen* is used also as an expression of gratitude and that it is used as often, or even more often than, *Arigatoo* or *Arigatoo-gozaimasu*. But he does not understand how *Sumimasen* compares with *Arigatoo(-gozaimasu)* when it is used to express gratitude.

* * *

Sumimasen.
すみません。

is used to express gratitude when one feels that one does not deserve a kindness or when one didn't expect it. When Mr. Lerner gave her son a present Mrs. Takada said *Sumimasen* because she had not expected it (or was not supposed to expect it). If she had said *Arigatoo-gozaimasu*, it would sound as if she had expected it. Her son was too young to feel that way, so he said

Arigatoo.
ありがとう。

Many Japanese feel that *Sumimasen* sounds more polite than *Arigatoo(-gozaimasu)*, but the difference is not simply in formality but in the speaker's psychological attitude. It depends on how the speaker feels about the kindness someone else has done for him whether he chooses *Sumimasen* or *Arigatoo(-gozaimasu)*.

Suppose you have noticed that someone has dropped something in the street and have called his attention to it. Some people will say *Sumimasen* and some will say *Arigatoo(-gozaimasu)* to you. Generally speaking, women are more likely to use *Sumimasen* than men. There is also a difference in generation in the usage of this expression, as well as other expressions. Young people use *Arigatoo(-gozaimasu)* more often while older people prefer *Sumimasen*.

From Mr. Lerner's Diary

June 22

During the coffee break today someone started complimenting Miss Yoshida on her becoming more beautiful these days, and everyone agreed. I joined them by saying

Watashi-ga kita-kara totemo kiree-ni narimashita-ne.

(She has become very beautiful because I came.)

What I really meant was that she had become very beautiful since the time I had come. I immediately realized that I had said *kita-kara* (because I came) when I should have said *kitekara* (after I came), but it was too late. Everybody thought it was very funny, except Miss Yoshida. I wanted to explain, but they wouldn't give me a chance.

I have to remember always to be careful with these two expressions.

······てから vs. ······たから

    *   *   *

June 29

Today Mr. Takada asked me about my uncle who had been ill for some time, so I answered that he had passed away a week ago. But when I said *Yatto shinimashita*, meaning "He finally passed away," Mr. Takada looked at me in a strange way and asked if I expected to inherit his money.

Sensee later explained that *yatto* is used when something that one has been looking forward to has finally been realized. It was certainly a mistake to say *yatto* instead of *tootoo*.

とうとう vs. やっと

    *   *   *

July 6

I had a toothache today and left the office an hour early. I met Miss Yoshida when I was leaving, so I tried to say:

Kyoo-wa byooin-e ikimasu-kara, kore-de . . .
(I'm going to the hospital today, so I'm leaving now.)

Miss Yoshida laughed so much that I forgot my toothache for a moment. I did it again! I really have trouble distinguishing *byoo* and *biyoo*. I know that I should try to pronounce *byo* as one syllable when saying *byo-o-i-n* (hospital), otherwise it will sound like *bi-yo-o-i-n* (beauty parlor).

In the same way, *ju-u* (gun) must be clearly distinguished from *ji-yu-u* (freedom).

びょういん（病院）——hospital
びよういん（美容院）——beauty parlor

From Mr. Lerner's Diary

July 1

I showed Miss Yoshida a picture of my aunt standing in front of her house. She remarked that the house seemed to be very old. I said,

Ee, furui-desu. Obasan-mo daibu furui-desu.

(Yes, the house is old. My aunt is fairly old, too.)

Miss Yoshida said that it was a clever joke, but I never meant it to be one. I didn't know at the time that *furui* is not used to refer to a person's age but that *toshi-o totte-iru* is used instead. When one says that someone is *furui*, that means *atama-ga furui*, namely his or her way of thinking is old-fashioned. So Miss Yoshida took my remark as subtly criticizing my aunt.

とし（を）　とっている　vs.　ふるい

Lack of knowledge of Japanese sometimes makes me an unwitting humorist.

*　　　*　　　*

July 8

During lunch hour I had some coffee with Mr. Takada at a coffee shop near the office. He asked for hot coffee but I wanted to have my coffee cold, so I said,

Samui-no kudasai (Give me a cold one.)

The waitress didn't understand. When Mr. Takada told her *Aisu-da-yo*, she immediately understood. Mr. Takada said I should have said *tsumetai* instead of *samui* to refer to coffee. I asked him why but he wasn't sure.

Sensee told me that *samui* is used to refer to the air while *tsumetai* is used for something that we can touch. In other words, *tsumetai* is tan-

108

gible — for example, *tsumetai te* (cold hand),
tsumetai kaze (cold wind), *tsumetai mizu* (cold
water), etc.

つめたい vs. さむい

But what about *tsumetai kokoro* (cold
heart), *tsumetai koe* (cold voice) or *tsumetai
taido* (cold attitude)? Are they tangible? *Sensee*
would not give in; he said these things are tangible in the Japanese imagination!

*   *   *

July 15
Business came up at the office that will take
Mr. Takada down to Hakata, Kyushu. Mr. Takada wondered, *Hakata-made dono-gurai kakaru-
deshoo.* (How much or how long will it take to
Hakata?) I said *Shinkansen-de niman'en-gurai-
deshoo*, meaning it will cost about ¥20,000 by
Shinkansen. Mr. Takada and the several other
people who were there said I was joking again,
but I wasn't. It was my mistake in pronouncing
the *n* sound. My sentence sounded like "It takes
twenty thousand years (*niman-nen*)" instead of
"twenty thousand yen (*niman'en*)." I have to be
careful not to touch the tongue to the roof of the
mouth when I pronounce the *n* sound preceding a
vowel like *e*, *o*, and others.

にまんえん（二万円） vs. にまんねん（二万年）

Sanjippun-shika arimasen-kara . . .

三十分しか　ありませんから……

(I only have 30 minutes, so . . .)

A few days ago Miss Yoshida asked Mr. Lerner if he could help her with something that day. Mr. Lerner was rather busy and could spare only 30 minutes to help her. Since he did not like to hurry with work, he said

Kyoo-wa sanjippun-dake arimasu-kara . . .

meaning "I only have 30 minutes today, so . . ." He expected Miss Yoshida to understand that he didn't have time to do it, but she again asked *Ja, yatte-kudasaru-n-desu-ne.* (Then you'll do it for me, won't you?) When Mr. Lerner said that he was busy that day and would rather do it the next day, Miss Yoshida left, looking a little confused.

Mr. Takada said later that Mr. Lerner should have said

Kyoo-wa sanjippun-shika arimasen-kara . . .
きょうは　三十分しか　ありませんから……

to mean that he only had 30 minutes so he couldn't do it.

*　　*　　*

Mr. Lerner had learned the expression ". . . *shika* plus the negative" which means "only . . .," but he thought that it meant the same thing as ". . . *dake* plus the affirmative" and had never used it very much.

The two expressions are not equivalent; . . . *dake* is used to indicate the exact amount, meaning "neither more nor less than . . ." while . . . *shika* . . . *nai* means that the amount referred to is very small or too small. Therefore if someone says *Sanjippun-shika arimasen-kara* the listener immediately understands that the time is so limited that the proposal cannot be accepted. On the other hand, if someone says *Sanjippun-dake arimasu-kara* it means that the speaker has exactly 30 minutes without clearly suggesting what follows. The speaker can mean that 30 minutes should be sufficient to do something completely or that he can do just a part of the plan. The important difference between . . . *dake aru* and . . . *shika nai* is that the former is not as suggestive, and the listener usually has to wait for the speaker to complete his sentence.

This difference is also true when money is involved. Saying *Juuman-en-shika arimasen-kara* means that the money is not enough to carry out a plan, while saying *Juuman-en-dake arimasu-kara* usually means that something can be done with the money, although what can be done is not yet clear.

When referring to your fluency in Japanese, if you want to emphasize that your knowledge of Japanese is small (regardless of how well you know it), you should say *Nihongo-wa sukoshi-shika dekimasen*, rather than *Nihongo-ga sukoshi-dake dekimasu*. Most Japanese will find the latter strange because they don't understand what you actually want to say.

Aizuchi-no uchikata

あいづちの　うちかた

(Giving the proper aizuchi)

Mr. Lerner has noticed that the Japanese often say *Hai, Ee, Soo-desu-ka* and other such words while listening to someone talking. *Sensee* told him that these short reply words are called "*aizuchi*" and are used to indicate that the listener has been listening attentively so far and wants the speaker to go on. In other words, *aizuchi* are something like a traffic signal that makes the flow of conversation smooth. As an ardent student of Japanese, Mr. Lerner recently made up his mind to give *aizuchi* himself although he found it rather hard to do.

This morning while talking with Mr. Okada on the phone, he tried hard to say *Hai* as often as possible, since Mr. Okada uses it very often himself. But it didn't work. When Mr. Lerner had said *Hai* several times, Mr. Okada suddenly stopped talking and said good-bye rather hurriedly. This was not like Mr. Okada, who always uses several sentences when parting.

Mr. Takada, who was nearby, noticed Mr. Lerner's confused look and said that his *Hai* had sounded as if he were asking Mr. Okada to stop talking.

*　　　*.　　　*

112

The word *Hai* is used as an *aizuchi* quite often; in fact, it is used even more often in giving *aizuchi* than in indicating agreement. Not only that, it is also used to indicate that you don't want to hear any more. It resembles the English "All right. All right. That's enough!" Mr. Lerner actually used *Hai* in this sense although he didn't in the least mean to.

When giving *aizuchi*, it is important to do it exactly when the speaker expects it. When the speaker is asking for *aizuchi* he slows down the last part of the phrase and says it with a dangling intonation. For instance, instead of saying *Kinoo odenwa-shimashita-ga* (I called yesterday, but), he says *Kinoo odenwa-shi-ma-shi-ta-ga. . .* If you give *aizuchi* before the speaker does this, he feels that you want him to stop talking. This is true of any *aizuchi* word, but *Hai* is most often used to show that someone wants the other to stop talking.

It is important to always choose the right moment in giving *aizuchi*, but one should especially be careful when talking on the phone. Since you cannot see each other, there is no way for your listener to know how you feel except by the way you talk.

From Mr. Lerner's Diary

July 20

During the coffee break this afternoon several people started talking about some frightening movie which has just come to Japan. I tried to go see it last weekend but I was too busy, so I said

Watashi-mo senshuu itte-mimashita.

meaning "I tried to go to it last week." Then Miss Yoshida eagerly asked me how I liked it. I felt a little confused but explained that I was too busy to go. Then she understood but I didn't understand my mistake in using the . . . *te-miru* form, so I asked *Sensee*.

He told me that *itte-miru* means "to go and see what will happen" and that if someone says *itte-mimashita* it means that he actually went somewhere. I should have said *ikoo-to shimashita* (I tried to go) or *ikoo-to omoimashita* (I thought I would go).

He gave me two very good example sentences to show the difference between *shiyoo-to suru* and *shite-miru*.

Kekkon-shiyoo-to shimashita-ga dame-deshita.

けっこんしようと しましたが だめでした。

(They tried to marry but couldn't.)

Kekkon-shite-mimashita-ga dame-deshita.
けっこんしてみましたが だめでした。

(They married — *lit.* to see what would happen — but it didn't work out.)

* * *

July 27

Mr. Takada was caught in a shower and came back to the office drenched to the skin. I happened to have an extra shirt, so I tried to say to him

> *Yokattara kite-kudasai.*
> (Please wear it if you'd like.)

I thought it was a perfect sentence, but he looked puzzled and did not say anything for a moment. Then he started laughing.

What I had actually said *Kitte-kudasai* (Please cut it) instead of *Kite-kudasai* (Please wear it).

As *Sensee* often tells me, I should try not to stress the *ki* sound when saying *kite*; otherwise it will sound like *kitte* to the Japanese ear. The same thing is true when saying *shite-imasu*; *shite-imasu* means "I'm doing" and *shitte-imasu* means "I know."

Sensee told me that when pronouncing *kite* or *shite* I should remember to make the *i* sound voiceless — namely pronounce it as if whispering it. Also, *kite* and *kitte* have different accents; the accent rises on the second syllable for *kite* and falls in the case of *kitte*.

きて（着て）ください。──Please wear it.
きって（切って）ください。──Please cut it.

Gokuroosama

ごくろうさま

(Thank you for your trouble)

Mr. Lerner wanted to send a Japanese doll to his mother for her birthday. When he asked Miss Yoshida about dolls during lunch time, she said she would go and buy one for him on her way home because she had a friend working in a doll shop. The next morning Miss Yoshida brought a beautiful doll in kimono to the office and handed it to Mr. Lerner. Mr. Lerner knew that she must have had a hard time carrying it on the crowded trains, so he said

Gokuroosama.
ごくろうさま。

(Thank you for your trouble.)

He meant it to be an expression of his gratitude, but Miss Yoshida didn't seem pleased. Mr. Takada also said that *Gokuroosama* was not appropriate in this situation.

* * *

Mr. Lerner was right in using *Gokuroosama* to express appreciation for Miss Yoshida's hard work, but he was wrong in using it when she had done something she was not expected to do as a duty.

116

Japanese use *Gokuroosama* most often to thank people for having rendered such service as delivering things or going on an errand; it is most often said to newspaper boys, porters, bell-boys, delivery men and the like. In such cases you might take this expression as a kind of verbal tip.

You should not say *Gokuroosama* to someone who has done something for you out of sheer kindness. For example, if someone picks up something you have dropped in the street, you should say *Arigatoo-gozaimasu* or *Sumimasen*; *Gokuroosama* will sound not only inappropriate but also very rude.

It is also wrong to say *Gokuroosama* to someone with whom you should speak politely. A teacher can show his appreciation of a student's hard work by saying *Gokuroosama*, but a student cannot say the same thing to his teacher. Teachers of Japanese often feel embarrassed when thanked by their students with *Gokuroosama*.

Gokuroosama implies the evaluation of someone's hard work by the speaker. Japanese feel it is not polite to evaluate one's superiors, even positively; therefore *Gokuroosama* is seldom used towards them.

However, it can be used regardless of the listener's status if it is used impersonally. For example, you will sometimes hear news reporters use it towards such people as the Prime Minister, delegation members, or participants in the Olympic Games on their return to Japan. In such cases *Gokuroosama* is directed to them not as individuals doing a favor for the speaker but as public servants working for the nation.

Soo yuu wake-desu-kara . . .

そう いう わけですから

(This is the situation, so . . .)

Yesterday afternoon, Mr. Lerner had some business to attend to outside of the office, and he told Mr. Takada that he was going out for about two hours. Mr. Takada looked at the clock and said

Ja, yoji-goro kaeru wake-desu-ne.
(So you're coming back around four?)

Mr. Lerner agreed but wondered why Mr. Takada had added *wake-desu-ne*. He thought that *wake* meant "reason" and felt its use strange when there was no particular reason for his coming back around four. He then remembered that Japanese use *wake* in a similar way very often — even more than necessary.

*   *   *

Wake is used in various ways. These can be divided into two usages. One is the usage in the sense of "reason" or "cause" as in

Wake-o hanashite-kudasai.
(Please tell me why.)

The other is the one that Mr. Takada used. In

118

this usage *wake* means "situation," and *wake-desu* is added to the main part of the sentence, seemingly changing the meaning very little. Mr. Takada could have simply said *Yoji-goro kaeri-masu-ne* without changing the meaning. Here *wake-desu* is added to show the speaker's attitude or emotion.

Wake here means "situation," and Mr. Takada's sentence can be paraphrased as "You're going out for two hours, and it is two now, so you're coming back around four — this is the situation you are in, right?" By adding *wake-desu*, the speaker shows that he has clarified the situation. Therefore, after explaining various reasons for being unable to do something, people often say

Soo yuu wake-desu-kara . . .
そう いう わけですから……

(*lit.* It is that kind of situation, meaning "Since this is the situation I'm in now, please understand.")

The listener in the above sentence will say

Aa, soo yuu wake-desu-ka. Ja, shikata-ga arimasen-ne.
(Is that the situation? Then it can't be helped.)

Thus he shows that he has come to share an understanding of the situation.

Kaettara sugu denwa-shimasu

かえったら　すぐ　電話します

(I'll call you as soon as I get home)

Mr. Takada wanted to have dinner with Mr. Lerner to introduce him to one of his friends, so he asked what evening he would be free the following week. But Mr. Lerner had left his engagement book at home that day, so he said

Watashi-ga kaettara sugu denwa-shimasu.
(I'll call you as soon as I get home.)

He thought that this was a perfect sentence, but Mr. Takada still gave him the look that he always had when Mr. Lerner's Japanese was a little strange.

        *   *   *

In this situation a Japanese would say

Kaettara sugu denwa-shimasu.
かえったら　すぐ　電話します。

Watashi-ga kaettara sugu denwa-shimasu would mean either that "I" will call rather than anyone else or that someone will call only after I return. In Mr. Lerner's case, there is no need to say *watashi*, including it sounds either strange or misleading.

Another example: when serving tea, a Japanese would not say *Doozo ocha-o nonde-kudasai*. Just *Doozo* or *Ocha-o doozo* is sufficient. *Doozo ocha-o nonde-kudasai* is used in other situation; the meaning will change depending on what word is emphasized.

Doozo OCHA-O nonde-kudasai.
(Please have tea rather than something else.)
Doozo ocha-o NONDE-KUDASAI.
(Please drink the tea rather than doing something else with it — throwing it away, for instance.)

Thus, when serving tea, it is correct to say *Doozo* or *Ocha-o doozo*.

Speakers of English tend to think that they should use a complete sentence — complete in the sense of the English equivalent — and try to say *Watashi-ga kaettara denwa-shimasu* or *Doozo ocha-o nonde-kudasai*. If they do this all the time, they give the impression either of sticking to classroom Japanese or being overly specific, boastful, or even aggressive. In order to properly communicate in Japanese, it is important to keep in mind that what seem to be grammatically complete sentences are not necessarily the best.

From Mr. Lerner's Diary

Aug. 22

I have noticed that people often say . . . *chatta*. *Sensee* explained that this is a contraction of . . .*te-shimatta* and that it means something is completely done. So I tried to use it to tell Mr. Takada that Miss Aoyama had gotten married I said

Aoyama-san-ga kekkon-shichatta-soo-desu.

Mr. Takada looked at me closely and asked if I had wanted to marry her.

I asked *Sensee* again. He explained that . . . *te-shimatta* (or . . .*chatta* in contraction) often implies that the speaker is unhappy about what has happened. So it is all right to say *heta-ni natte-shimatta* (I have become poor at it) but it is not proper to say *joozu-ni natte-shimatta* (I have become good at it) except in special cases. Saying *Aoyama-san-ga kekkon-shite-shimatta-soo-desu* implies that I am somehow unhappy about her marriage. I should have simply said

Aoyama-san-ga kekkon-shita-soo-desu.

After listening to *Sensee*'s explanation I said

Mata shippai-shichatta.
また しっぱいしちゃった。
(I made a mistake again.)

and he praised my sentence!

*   *   *

Aug. 29

A couple of weeks ago I named Mr. Kato "Mr. *Maa-ne*" (Mr. Kind-of). Miss Yoshida said it was a very good nickname and admired my Japanese. Perhaps I am more sensitive to people's favorite phrases than most Japanese as a foreigner learning Japanese.

The word *maa*, I understand, is used to express agreement with some reservation. Sometimes *Ee, maa* (Well, yes) can be more considerate than the more direct *Ee, soo-desu* (Yes, that's so). But Mr. Kato uses it too much. He starts every sentence with *maa*. When someone asks him for permission to do something, he says *Maa, ii-deshoo* (Well, I guess it's all right). When someone asks if he wants something, he says *Maa-ne*. In such cases, Miss Yoshida says it is much better to say *Ee* or *Ee, ii-desu-yo*.

I have wanted for some time to make him say *Ee* or *Iie* without using *maa*. Since most Japanese strongly deny any compliment, I thought it would be a good idea to compliment him on something. Today I noticed that he had a new watch, so I complimented him on it, expecting him to say *Iie!*

But it didn't work. He said

Ee, maa-ne . . . Nedan-no wari-niwa-ne.
ええ、まあね……ねだんの　わりにはね。
(Well, yes — for its price.)

123

Kowashimashita

こわしました

(I broke it)

The other evening Mr. Lerner dropped in at the Takadas' for a cup of tea and had a chance to observe an interesting conversation between Mrs. Takada and one of her neighbors.

The neighbor had borrowed the Takadas' camera, but something went wrong with it. The neighbor blamed herself, saying

Kowashite-shimaimashite. . .
こわしてしまいまして……
(I ended up breaking it, so. . .)

and Mrs. Takada also blamed herself, saying

Iie, motomoto chooshi-ga yoku nakatta-n-desu-kara. . .
(No, it wasn't in good condition from the beginning.)

After a long discussion they finally decided that each of them would pay half of the repair costs.

What Mr. Lerner felt interesting was that the two women kept blaming themselves; but then when he thought again, he felt most Japanese always seem to be blaming themselves more than necessary.

*　　*　　*

One of the American students we know once had this kind of experience. But when she returned the heater she had borrowed, she said *Kowaremashita* (It broke) instead of saying *Kowashimashita* (I broke it); at this point her landlady stopped being friendly to her.

This tendency to try to be polite by blaming oneself is common in Japan. It is well known that the Japanese often say when giving a present

>*Tsumaranai mono-desu-ga*
>(It is a very trifling thing, but);

they say when offering food

>*Okuchi-ni aimasen-deshoo-ga*
>(*lit*. It won't suit your palate, but).

The Japanese feel that consideration or respect towards others should not be limited to the persons themselves, but should be extended to their belongings as well. Therefore Mrs. Takada's neighbor blamed herself for what had happened to the camera she had borrowed.

But this is seen only when the two people are, or want to be, on good terms with one another. Relations between tenants and landlords at present have changed from the past, but some landlords still feel that tenants are like their family members. The landlady would not have felt offended by the American girl who said *Kowaremashita* if she had not wanted to be on good terms with her.

From Mr. Lerner's Diary

Sept. 9

Why don't Japanese end their sentences more clearly with either *desu* or *ja arimasen*? I really have trouble figuring out whether they are in the affirmative or in the negative.

Today, when we were discussing some movie during the coffee break at the office, Miss Yoshida said,

Are, omoshiroku nai-n-ja nai?

I found out later that she meant it wasn't very interesting, but when I first heard her say this, I thought she meant it was interesting because double negation means affirmative.

Sensee told me that I should keep in mind that such sentence endings as . . .*n-ja nai?* or . . .*n-ja nai-deshoo-ka* (more polite) have no substantial meaning but are just added to convey the speaker's emotion.

Next time I'll try saying,

Waruku nai-n-ja nai-deshoo-ka
(It's not bad, is it?)

instead of directly saying *Waruku arimasen* and see if Miss Yoshida will notice my progress in Japanese.

······んじゃ　ないでしょうか。

*　　　*　　　*

Sept. 16

This evening when I was leaving the office, I noticed that Mr. Takada was looking for something. When I asked him about it, I thought that he said,

Kani-o sagashite-iru-n-desu.
(I'm looking for a crab.)

So I willingly joined this exciting search. But after some time Mr. Takada said *A atta, atta* (I found it), showing me a small key.

When I told *Sensee* this, he said that the *g* sound in the word *kagi* is usually nasalized so that the *gi* sounds similar to *ni*. This is why I mistook *kagi* (key) for *kani* (crab).

Sensee explained that the *g* sound is usually nasalized unless it comes at the beginning of a word; the two *g* sounds in such phrases as *gakkoo-ga* are actually quite different although written with the same *hiragana* or *roomaji*.

He went on and explained that some people are against making this distinction while many people, especially teachers of Japanese and teachers of music, strongly favor it because the nasalized *g* sounds more pleasant to them.

I don't know whether it sounds better or worse, but I'd rather Japanese didn't nasalize the noninitial *g* because it makes it hard for me to distinguish *kagi* from *kani* and *kugi* (nail) from *kuni* (country).

Dekiru-kashira

できるかしら

(I wonder if you can do it)

A few days ago Mr. Lerner heard Mr. Sato ask Miss Yoshida

Kore ashita-made-ni dekiru-kashira.
これ　あしたまでに　できるかしら。
(I wonder if you can do this by tomorrow.)

Mr. Lerner was a little surprised because he had heard that . . .*kashira* was used by women. Then, when Miss Yoshida said that she couldn't do it because she had something else to do, Mr. Sato said, to double Mr. Lerner's surprise,

Aa, kyoo-wa isogashii-no-ne.
(Oh, you're busy today, aren't you?)

again using a feminine expression. Mr. Sato is about 40, tall and well-built; he is not at all feminine or sissy. Why did he use women's expressions?

*　　*　　*

In familiar speech men and women use some different words and expressions. Such expressions as . . .*kashira* and . . .*no-ne* are usually used by women, but there are cases where men

128

also use them.

Mr. Sato would not normally say . . .*kashira* or . . .*no-ne* to men of his own age; he would use these expressions only when talking to young people, especially young women. He would not have said . . .*kashira* or . . .*no-ne* if Miss Yoshida were older than he. The age, not only the sex, of the listener often determines the tone of speech.

When talking with children, both men and women tend to use children's speech. Women teachers in kindergartens or elementary schools, for example, often say something like

> *Mata issho-ni ikoo-ne.*
> (Let's go together again, shall we?)

adopting children's speech. They would never talk in the same way to the children's parents.

Old people are sometimes talked to as if they were young children. Japanese usually try to be polite towards older people, but they often talk to people whom they regard as very old and therefore weak as if talking to children. When giving a seat to an old woman on the train, for example, a man may use a familiar expression.

> *Obaachan, koko-e kakenasai-yo.*
> (Come and sit down here, Granny.)

Most old people seem to accept this as a matter of fact while some dislike it as unnecessarily patronizing — people are as old as they feel.

We might say that the stronger one often changes his tone in accordance with the weaker one — if men can be considered as stronger than women and adults as stronger than children or old people.

129

Uchi-wa motto hidoi-n-desu-yo

うちは　もっと　ひどいんですよ

(It's worse for us)

Mr. Okada, who often comes to Mr. Lerner's office on business, had recently built his own house. Several people at the office congratulated him on this and said they wished they were so lucky. Mr. Okada thanked them but would not admit that he was happy about his new house. He just kept complaining saying that he had to pay back a lot of money, that he had to spend more time commuting, that keeping the garden clean took so much time, and so on. It sounded as if he had done a terrible thing in building a house. Mr. Lerner who had been listening intently ended up feeling very sorry for him and so said,

Soo-desu-ka. Sore-wa ikemasen-ne.
(Is that so? That's too bad.)

Then the people who were there started laughing; Mr. Okada looked embarrassed and left hurriedly. What was wrong with expressing sympathy for poor Mr. Okada?

*　　　*　　　*

The Japanese often complain about their ill luck to others; they do not usually admit their good luck easily. It may be partly from consid-

130

eration for the feelings of others or from a fear of arousing coldness or enmity. And on the listeners' side as well, they usually do not admit the speaker's ill luck but keep on praising or envying; thus Mr. Lerner's expression of sympathy seemed rather out of place in the above-mentioned case.

Complaining about one's family members is a popular topic among Japanese, especially among women. Mothers usually complain about their children's bad manners and poor school grades; wives complain that their husbands are lazy and inconsiderate. The listener usually says that her children or husband is even worse. After confirming through this kind of exchange that both of them are suffering the same kind of misfortune and have many things in common, they say their good-byes and forget all about it.

This is a pattern that is commonly seen in Japan but not always understood in other societies. A young Japanese woman we know once lived in the United States with her husband for about a year. Once when she attended a meeting in the neighborhood, she complained about her husband's being inconsiderate to her as she had often done in Japan. But the neighbors did not take this as a pattern of communication. Some women called up her husband and scolded him; some women asked her if she was looking for a boyfriend. It was her mistake to have expected the same reaction as she would have gotten from Japanese women, who would say

Otaku-wa ii hoo-desu-yo.
(Your husband is not very bad.)

or

Uchi-wa motto hidoi-n-desu-yo.
うちは もっと ひどいんですよ。
(My husband is worse.)

Nihongo-ga ojoozu-desu-ne

日本語が　おじょうずですね

(You speak Japanese very well)

One thing recently bothering Mr. Ernest Lerner is that Japanese are too ready to praise his Japanese. When he says *Hajimemashite* instead of "How do yo do?" to introduce himself, they look surprised; when he says *Ii otenki-desu-ne* (It's a nice day), they say *Raanaa-san, nihongo-ga ojoozu-desu-ne* (You speak Japanese very well, Mr. Lerner). If someone is complimented on his English for just being able to say "How do you do?" and "It's a nice day," he would feel ridiculed. Being able to say two short sentences or phrases does not mean that one is good at the language.

Mr. Lerner sometimes suspects that Japanese regard foreigners as hopelessly poor at language learning.

*　　　*　　　*

It is easy and comfortable for anyone to talk with those who belong to the same group, but it requires some effort to speak to someone outside the group. This is especially true with people who sharply distinguish those "inside" from those "outside." Therefore most Japanese want to have certain exchanges before they can feel at home with a foreigner. These exchanges consist

132

of certain questions and answers, or certain compliments and responses. Some typical questions are:

> *Okuni-wa dochira-desu-ka.*
> (Where are you from?)
> *Nihon-ryoori-wa taberaremasu-ka.*
> (Can you eat Japanese food?)
> *Nihon-wa nagai-desu-ka.*
> (Have you been in Japan a long time?)

And a typical compliment is

> **Nihongo-ga ojoozu-desu-ne.**
> 日本語が　おじょうずですね。
> (You speak Japanese very well.)

These questions and compliments are similar to "How do you do?" in that they are used to confirm that the speaker and the listener are opening communications rather than to gain information.

The Japanese are not always being nosey or flattering; these questions and compliments are very often manifestations of their determination to step outside their own group and approach a foreigner, a step which requires a great deal of courage from most Japanese. The effort underlying this kind of exchange should be properly appreciated. This appreciation will help break up what many foreigners feel as a barrier between themselves and the Japanese.

Benkyoo-ni narimashita

勉強に　なりました

(I learned from it)

Mr. Mori, the director of the company where Mr. Lerner works, published a short article about business administration in a certain magazine. Mr. Lerner read it and thought it was very good. So when he met Mr. Mori a few days ago he told him that he had read it and added

Taihen joozu-ni kakimashita.
(It's very well done — *lit.* You wrote it very well.)

But Mr. Mori did not seem to be pleased. Apparently Mr. Lerner's compliment was not appropriately expressed in Japanese.

*　　*　　*

American students sometimes come to their teacher of Japanese after class and say something like "You taught well" or "I liked the way you taught." The teachers feel rather embarrassed because although they feel happy about being evaluated highly, at the same time they have to tell their students that they should not express their admiration in such direct phrases to their seniors.

Most people refrain from directly evaluating their superiors either negatively or positively. They try to choose the proper occasion and the appropriate expression to indicate their evaluation of superiors. It is easier to evaluate one's superiors in some situations; in a familiar, friendly atmosphere one can be more free in evaluating one's superiors than in a serious or formal situation.

When one wants to praise one's superior on a serious occasion, one has to be careful to choose indirect, subtle expressions. If someone wants to praise his superior's work or achievement as Mr. Lerner did, one way to express it is to thank him by saying

Taihen benkyoo-ni narimashita.
たいへん　勉強に　なりました。
(I learned a great deal from it — *lit.* It became a good study.)
or
Taihen tame-ni narimashita.
(It taught me a great deal — *lit.* It did me a lot of good.)

Another way is to express your desire to read or hear more about it. After listening to a lecture people often say that they would like to hear the same speaker again some other time. Sometimes they use their wives to emphasize their admiration:

Nyooboo-nimo kikasete-yaritai-to omoimashita.
(I wish my wife were here to listen to you.)

An expression of thanks can also be used to indicate a student's admiration of his teacher. In this case,

Okagesama-de yoku wakarimashita.
(Thanks to your teaching, I understood well.)

is used most often.

Ee, maa, nantoka

ええ、まあ、なんとか

(Well, somehow I manage)

Mr. Lerner finds it difficult to respond to what Japanese say to him for the sake of politeness. A few days ago Mr. Saito praised his Japanese, so Mr. Lerner said as he had been told by *Sensee*

Iie, mada-mada-desu.
(No, I'm not any good at it yet — *lit.* No, not yet.)

Then Mr. Saito admired this response so much that Mr. Lerner had to say something else, so he said

Boku-nanka dame-desu-yo.
(I'm so poor at it — *lit.* Such a person as me is no good.)

Mr. Saito still kept praising him so lavishly that Mr. Lerner said, in a desperate struggle to stop him,

Soo-desu-ka. Doomo arigatoo.
(Is that right? Thank you.)

This succeeded in stopping him, but Mr. Lerner felt that somehow he had done something wrong.

When he asked Mr. Takada about it, he said that he should have ended the topic quickly by saying

Ee, maa, nantoka.
ええ、まあ、なんとか。
(Well, somehow I manage.)

* * *

Japanese usually strongly deny any praise. (It is different between good friends.) But there are cases when it is difficult to simply deny someone's praise. For instance, when someone congratulates you on an achievement such as publishing a book or opening a store, it is not quite appropriate to say *lie*. There are ways of partially admitting the praise:

Ee, maa, nantoka.
(Well, I managed to do it somehow.)
Maa, okagesama-de nantoka.
(Thanks to everybody I could manage.)
Maa, koko-made-wa nantoka.
(I have managed so far.)
Dooyara kooyara.
(Somehow or other.)

These expressions show that you have achieved something with much difficulty and that the achievement is not at all satisfactory.

If you feel it is too hypocritical to deny completely your acquaintance's praise about your Japanese, you can say

Okagesama-de nantoka sukoshi-wa wakaru-yoo-ni natte-kimashita.

(Thanks to you, I am beginning to understand a little bit.)

137

From Mr. Lerner's Diary

Oct. 20

Mr. Okada came to see me at the office this afternoon. I thought of calling a nearby coffee shop to have some coffee brought in, so I asked Mr. Okada about it. He said,

Kekkoo-desu.
けっこうです。

I thought that *Kekkoo-desu* meant "It's fine," so I immediately started dialing, but he looked surprised and hurriedly said,

Anoo, kekkoo-desu. Doozo okamai-naku.

I knew that *Doozo okamai-naku* means "Don't bother," so I guessed that Mr. Okada had used *Kekkoo-desu* to mean "No, thank you."

Sensee explained that *Kekkoo-desu* is used very often to decline someone's offer, sometimes with *iie* and sometimes without it. I wondered if any ambiguity is caused by using the same word both in the sense of "Yes, it's fine" and "No, thank you." He said Japanese usually don't get confused because they use other expressions when they want to accept an offer, and even when they use the word *kekkoo* they add *-ne* and say *Kekkoo-desu-ne.*

*   *   *

Oct. 27

To me Japanese seem to be saying . . .*ne* all the time, so I thought that . . .*ne* could be added to any sentence. But today Mr. Takada said my . . .*ne* sounded strange somehow when I said,

138

Watashi-wa kaeri-ni tomodachi-ni aimashita-ne.

meaning "I met a friend of mine on my way home from the office, you know."

Sensee said that I shouldn't say . . .*ne* when explaining what the listener does not know because . . .*ne* is used when the speaker expects the listener to share the same knowledge or feelings about something. In the above case no particle is necessary at the end unless you want to use . . .*yo* for emphasis.

But don't teachers often use . . .*ne* when explaining things to their students? *Sensee* answered that this is because teachers expect their students to feel as if they share the knowledge with the teacher. The more enthusiastic the teacher is, the more often he uses . . .*ne*.

......ねo

139

Itsudemo ii-desu
いつでも いいです

(Any time will do)

Mr. Lerner and Mr. Takada discussed some business with Mr. Saito for about an hour. When they were about to leave, Mr. Takada asked Mr. Saito when they could meet again. Mr. Saito said,

> *Itsudemo ii-desu.*
> いつでも いいです。
> (Any time will do.)

But when Mr. Takada asked if Friday would be all right, he said,

> *Kin'yoobi-wa chotto . . .*
> (Friday won't do — *lit.* As for Friday, it's a little . . .)

Mr. Lerner wanted to remind him that he had said any day would do, but Mr. Takada quickly said,

> *Ja, mokuyoobi-wa doo-deshoo.*
> (Then how about Thursday?)

Mr. Lerner did not quite understand this procedure. If Friday was inconvenient for Mr. Saito, why didn't he say from the beginning *Kin'yoobi-igai-wa ii-desu* (Any day will do except Friday)? He was either being inaccurate or indecisive, wasn't he?

*   *   *

Many Japanese say that any time will be good or anything will suit them when the decision

140

involves the listener's convenience. Telling precisely what day will be inconvenient is certainly more efficient, but many Japanese feel it is impolite to be specific about their own convenience. Therefore if you ask them what day will suit them, they will answer

Itsudemo ii-desu. (Any time will do.)

Suppose you offer a Japanese a meal; they will first say

Nandemo ii-desu. (Anything will do.)

But when you try to make sure if beefsteak is really OK, they may say

Bifuteki-wa chotto . . .
(*lit.* As for beefsteak, it's a little . . .)

Fried chicken or fried pork may not do either, and it may turn out that actually the Japanese guest wants nothing but *sashimi.*

Some Japanese may also think as Mr. Lerner did, that it is impolite to say at first that any day is fine and then say that a certain day is not right. They think it is more polite to say what day is inconvenient from the beginning.

But according to many Japanese, it is better not to say clearly from the outset what day is inconvenient. If the proposed time or choice suits them, that's fine; if it doesn't they can show hesitation by saying . . .*wa chotto* . . . and wait for another proposition, which will immediately be offered. The underlying idea behind this procedure is that it is not good manners to force the other to consider one's own convenience.

Understanding this different concept of politeness will make for smoother communication.

141

Osabishii-deshoo-ne

おさびしいでしょうね

(You must be lonely)

Recently Mr. Lerner's sister Margaret came to Japan to visit, and stayed with him for several weeks. After having a very good time, she left a few days ago. When he met Mr. Okada the next day and said that she had left, he said

Osabishii-deshoo-ne.
おさびしいでしょうね。
(You must be lonely.)

Mr. Lerner felt tempted to say *lie, betsu-ni* (No, not particularly). If Margaret were his wife or a girlfriend, he would have felt very lonely for her, but a grown up brother does not usually miss his sister so much. But he somehow felt he shouldn't say no, so he answered *Doomo* according to what he thought to be Japanese custom. This seemed to satisfy Mr. Okada, and he soon changed the subject.

But Mr. Okada was not the only compassionate acquaintance; almost everyone he met asked about Margaret and said *Osabishii-deshoo-ne*. Mr. Lerner could not help wondering why Japanese expect others to be lonely for their family.

*　　　*　　　*

142

This expression of sympathy is usually said to someone who is left behind by his family members, whether he is grown up or very young. To a parent whose daughter has left to get married, one usually says,

Omedetoo-gozaimasu. (Congratulations.)
as well as
Osabishii-deshoo-ne.

This is not said to the daughter.

In such cases as Mr. Lerner's, a person might say in English "It's nice that she could come to Japan," or "Too bad she couldn't stay longer." These expressions can be said among the Japanese, too, but it is customary and polite to show sympathy for Mr. Lerner's being lonely. A Westerner may take this expression as too personal or out of place towards an adult, but it is accepted as quite natural in Japan.

To this expression of sympathy, Japanese usually respond by saying *Hai, arigatoo-gozaimasu* and add such phrases as:

Demo, moo naremashita.
(But I'm accustomed to it.)
Demo, dandan narete-kuru-deshoo.
(But I'll get used to it.)

Soo-desu-ne

そうですね

(Well . . .)

Mr. Lerner listened while Mr. Takada was carefully explaining a proposal to Mr. Saito. Mr. Saito listened attentively, giving frequent *aizuchi*. When Mr. Takada had finished his explanation, Mr. Saito said

Soo-desu-ne.
そうですね。

Mr. Lerner thought this meant "That's right," and expected him to say *Ja, soo shimashoo.* But Mr. Saito said *Ja, moo ichido kangaete-mimasu* (I'll think it over), and left. Mr. Takada said that Mr. Saito would not accept their proposal. Mr. Lerner did not understand why he had said *Soo-desu-ne* first. But when he listened to Japanese talking, he noticed that they often start their replies with *Soo-desu-ne* regardless of what follows. They say

Soo-desu-ne. Yappari yamemashoo.
(*lit.* That's right. I won't do that.)
Soo-desu-ne. Yoku wakarimasen.
(*lit.* That's right. I don't understand it well.)

144

It seemed to Mr. Lerner that this *Soo-desu-ne* doesn't mean anything; it just shows that the speaker is going to give his reply.

*   *   *

Soo-desu-ne is used to show that the speaker has understood what has been asked and is going to reply to it. (*Ee* and *Hai* are also often used in this way.) In this sense, it is similar to "Well" in such sentences as "Well, I think . . ." In polite speech Japanese use *Soo-desu-ne* and in familiar speech they say *Soo-da-ne* (male) or *Soo-nee* (usually female).

It is said in a different tone when it doesn't mean "That's right." When it means "That's right," it is said with a falling tone like

So

o

-desu-ne.

When it is used to solicit agreement, meaning "That's right, don't you think?", it is said with a rising tone on the *ne* as

So

o   -ne?

-desu

When it is used to mean "Well, . . ." it is said with a dangling tone as

So

o

-desu-nee. . .

This is different from *Eeto* although both can be translated as "Well." *Eeto* is used when one cannot think of the right word, while *Soo-desu-ne* is usually intentionally used to avoid the abruptness which might be caused by giving the answer immediately. To prove this, children seldom use *Soo-desu-ne* or *Soo-da-ne* but they often use *Eeto*.

Otagaisama-desu

おたがいさまです

(It's the same for both of us)

About a week ago Mr. Lerner had a cup of coffee with Mr. Okada after discussing some business. Mr. Okada said that he had a lot of work to do at the office so it was very hard for him to take a vacation. When Mr. Lerner said that it was the same for him, Mr. Okada said

Otagaisama-desu-ne.
おたがいさまですね。

Mr. Lerner knew that *tagai* meant "mutual," but he was not familiar with this expression and thought he would ask someone about it later. But just that night when he was watching TV, a professional entertainer (called *tarento* — talent — in Japanese) said to another entertainer

Otagai-ni isogashii-kara-ne
(*lit.* We're mutually busy, so . . .)

obviously meaning "Both of us are busy, so . . ." Mr. Lerner suddenly remembered what Mr. Okada had said and realized that he had meant the same thing.

*　　　*　　　*

The word *tagai* or *otagai* by itself means "mutual." When you thank someone for his help, he may answer you

    Otagaisama-desu.

meaning that you don't have to feel particularly obligated because human beings should help each other.

    Human beings sometimes make trouble for each other instead of helping each other. For example, when a wife gets angry with the neighbor's noise and wants to tell them to be quiet, her husband may say

    Otagaisama-da-yo.

meaning that they themselves might be causing their neighbors some unpleasantness, so they should try to put up with the noise.

    Otagai sometimes means "both of us," as Mr. Okada and the entertainer on TV used it. Two people often say when parting

    Otagai-ni karada-ni ki-o tsukemashoo.
    (Let's both of us take care of ourselves.)
or
    Otagai-ni ganbarimashoo.
    (Let's both of us try hard.)

    Elderly people (or those who feel elderly) often say to each other

    Otagai-ni toshi-desu-kara-ne
    (Both of us are not so young any more, so . . .)

implying that they shouldn't overwork themselves or that they don't have to work as hard as

147

they used to.

Thus the expression *otagaisama* or *otagai-ni* is used to emphasize that the speaker and the listener share the same experience.

Otagai-ni kuroo-shimasu-nee (Both of us have a hard time, don't we?) is often used to comfort each other. The two may be husbands whose wives are poor housekeepers or wives whose husbands are lazy and of little help at home. Or, the two may be a Japanese who is learning English and a foreigner who is learning Japanese.

COMMON EXPRESSIONS USED
IN DAILY LIFE

Some of the expressions appearing here are explained in the main text of this book. In such cases please see the page indicated in parentheses.

When more than one expression with the same meaning are listed, the more common ones are first.

There are many different expressions depending on the degree of politeness or formality; the ones listed here are most common.

GREETINGS USED WHEN MEETING PEOPLE
☐ **introducing others**

Kochira-wa Tanaka-san-desu. (This is Mr. Tanaka.)

Kanai-desu. (This is my wife.)

Shujin-desu. (This is my husband.)

☐ **meeting for the first time**

Hajimemashite. (How do you do? — *lit.* It's the first time.) (cf. p.132)

Doozo yoroshiku. (Glad to meet you. — *lit.* Please be good to me.) (cf. p.75)

(These two expressions are sometimes used together.)

Shujin-ga itsumo osewa-ni natte-orimasu. (You're very kind to my husband — *lit.* My husband is always taken care of by you.) (cf. p. 76)

☐ **meeting again**

Senjitsu-wa shitsuree-shimashita. (*lit.* I was rude when I met you the other day.) (cf. p. 46)

Senjitsu-wa doomo. (*lit.* Thank you for the other day.)

Senjitsu-wa gochisoosama-deshita. (*lit.* Thank you for the feast the other day.) (cf. p. 46)

□depending on the time of day

Ohayoo-gozaimasu. (Good morning. — *lit.* It's early.) (cf. p.17)

Konnichiwa. (Good afternoon. Hello. — *lit.* This day is . . .) (cf. p. 16)

Konbanwa. (Good evening. — *lit.* This evening is . . .) (cf. p.17)

Oyasuminasai. (Good night. — *lit.* Please take a rest.)

(These greetings cannot be used to mean "Good-bye" in the same way that the English equivalents are sometimes used.)

□referring to the weather

Ii otenki-desu-ne. (It's a nice day, isn't it? — *lit.* It's good weather.)

Atsui-desu-ne. (It's hot, isn't it?)

Samui-desu-ne. (It's cold, isn't it?)

Ii yooki-desu-ne. (It's a nice season, isn't it?)

Suzushiku narimashita-ne. (It has become nice and cool, hasn't it?)

Atatakaku narimashita-ne. (It has become nice and warm, hasn't it?)

Yoku furimasu-ne. (It rains a lot, doesn't it?)

Hakkiri-shimasen-ne. (We don't know how the weather will change. — *lit.* It hasn't made up its mind.)

□asking about health

(Asking about the listener's health is not as common as in English. The following questions sound more personal than "How are you?")

Ogenki-desu-ka. (How are you? — *lit.* Are you well?)

Okawari arimasen-ka. (How are you? — *lit.* Hasn't there been any change?)

Minasan, okawari arimasen-ka. (How's everybody? — *lit.* Hasn't there been any change with all of you?)

Ikaga-desu-ka. (How are you?) (cf. p. 24)

□**answers to inquiry about health**

Okagesama-de (genki-desu). (Thanks to you, I'm fine. — *lit.* Thanks to everyone and everything, I'm fine.) (cf. p. 72)

Okagesama-de daibu yoku narimashita. (I'm better, thank you. — *lit.* Thanks to everything that has helped me, I have become better.) (cf. p.135)

□**meeting on special occasions**

Akemashite omedetoo-gozaimasu. (Happy New Year! — *lit.* We are happy that New Year's Day has dawned.) (cf. p. 52)

Shinnen omedetoo-gozaimasu. (Happy New Year! — *lit.* We are happy to have the New Year.)(cf. pp.50, 53)

Sakunen-chuu-wa iroiro osewasama-ni narimashita. (Thank you for many things you did for me last year.) (cf. p. 53)

Honnen (or Kotoshi)-mo yoroshiku onegai-itashimasu. (— *lit.* Please be kind to me this year, too.) (cf. p. 53)

Doozo yoi otoshi-o. (Happy New Year! — *lit.* Please meet a good year.) (cf. p. 50)

PARTING

Dewa, shitsuree-itashimasu. (Good-bye. — *lit.* I'm going to be rude.) (cf. p.69)

Sayoonara. (Good-bye.)

Dewa (or Ja), mata. (See you later. — *lit.* Then, again.)

□**to someone who is sick**

Doozo odaiji-ni. (Please take good care of yourself. — *lit.* Please be careful.) (cf. p. 51)

□**to someone who is going out**

Itte-rasshai. (Have a good time — *lit.* Go and come back.) (cf. pp.51, 62)

(Doozo) oki-o tsukete. (Take care. — *lit.* (Please be careful.) (cf. p. 51)

151

☐**asking to pass on one's regards**

Okusan-ni yoroshiku. (Please give my regards to your wife. — *lit.* Please say well to your wife.)

EXPRESSING GRATITUDE

Arigatoo-gozaimasu. (Thank you very much.)

Arigatoo. (Thanks.)

Arigatoo-gozaimashita. (Thank you very much. — *lit.* Thank you for what you have done for me.)

Osewasama-de gozaimashita. (Thank you for your kindnesses. — *lit.* You have taken care of me.) (cf. p. 76)

Gokuroosama. (Thank you for your trouble.) (cf. p.116)

Doomo. (Thanks. — *lit.* Very.) (*Doomo* is added for emphasis with any of the expressions of gratitude.) (cf. p. 22)

APOLOGIES

(Apologies can often be used as expressions of gratitude.)

Sumimasen. (I'm sorry. Thank you.) (cf. p. 104)

Doomo sumimasen. (I'm very sorry. Thank you very much.)

☐**for taking someone's time**

Ojama-shimashita. (I'm sorry I took your time — *lit.* I interrupted you.) (cf. p. 68)

☐**for asking someone's help**

Otesuu-o kakemashita. (*lit.* I caused you trouble.)

Gomendoo-o kakemashita. (*lit.* I caused you trouble.)

☐**for troubling someone**

Gomeewaku-o okake-shimashita. (I'm sorry I bothered you.)

152

□for not seeing (or writing) someone

Gobusata-itashimashita. (*lit.* I haven't seen (or written) you for a long time.) (cf. p. 75)

□for being late

Osoku natte sumimasen. (I'm sorry to be late.)

□for leaving

Sorosoro shitsuree-itashimasu. (I'd like to be excused. — *lit.* I'm going to be rude now.)

Osaki-ni shitsuree-itashimasu. (Please excuse me. — *lit.* I'm rude enough to leave before you.)

REPLIES TO EXPRESSIONS OF GRATITUDE AND APOLOGIES

Iie. (No.) (cf. p. 10)

Iie, doo-itashimashite. (No, not at all.)

Ii-n-desu-yo. (That's all right.)

Tondemonai. (Nothing of the sort.)

Kochira-koso. (I should be the one to say so.) (cf. pp.74, 76)

Kamaimasen-yo. (I don't mind.)

EXPRESSIONS OF SYMPATHY AND EMPATHY

(Expressions of sympathy and empathy are considered to be polite; they are not felt to be patronizing or intrusive.)

□for hard work

Taihen-desu-ne. (It's tough. — *lit.* It's terrible, isn't it?) (cf. p. 64)

Otsukaresama. (It's tough. — *lit.* You must be tired.)

□for misfortune

Sore-wa ikemasen-ne. (That's too bad.)

Taihen-deshita-ne. (It was tough.)

Zannen-deshita-ne. (That's too bad. — *lit.* It was regrettable.)

□for bereavement
Kono tabi-wa tonda koto-de . . . (I'm very sorry to hear it. — *lit*. This time, it was an awful thing.)

Okuyami-mooshiagemasu. (My deepest condolences.)

Osasshi-itashimasu. (My deepest condolences. — *lit*. I can imagine how you feel.)

□for being left by family members
Osabishii-deshoo-ne. (*lit*. You must be lonely.) (cf. p.142)

□for being worried
Sore-wa goshinpai-deshoo. (*lit*. You must be worried about it.)

□for being in trouble
Sore-wa okomari-deshoo. (*lit*. You must be inconvenienced by that.)

□for happiness
Omedetoo-gozaimasu. (Congratulations.) (cf. p.143)

Yokatta-desu-ne. (I'm glad to hear that. — *lit*. It was good.)

Sore-wa naniyori-desu-ne. (I'm glad to hear that. — *lit*. That's better than anything else.)

Oyorokobi-mooshiagemasu. (Congratulations. — *lit*. I express my pleasure.)

□for anticipating something good
Otanoshimi-desu-ne. (*lit*. You're looking forward to it, aren't you?) (This is said to a person who has promising children or who is nearing the completion of his work, etc.)

EXPRESSIONS OF APPROVAL
Kekkoo-desu. (Fine.) (cf. p.138)
Sore-wa ii-desu-ne. (That's good.)
Sansee-desu. (I agree.)
Daisansee-desu. (I heartily agree.)
Sono toori-desu-ne. (Exactly.)

EXPRESSIONS OF DISAPPROVAL

Sore-wa doo-deshoo-ne. (I have some doubts about that. — *lit.* How is that, I wonder.)

Chotto muri-deshoo-ne. (It's not quite right. — *lit.* It will probably be a little unreasonable.)

Soo-demo nai-deshoo. (Not quite. — *lit.* It probably isn't so.)

ASKING FAVORS

Chotto onegai-ga aru-n-desu-ga. (I have a little favor to ask of you.) (cf. p. 81)

Kore, onegai-shimasu. (Please take care of this. — *lit.* I ask this of you.) (cf. p. 59)

Yoroshiku onegai-shimasu. (Please do this. — *lit.* I ask you to do it kindly.) (cf. p. 59)

Zehi onegai-shimasu. (Please, by all means, do it.)

DECLINING
□a favor

Chotto . . . (*lit.* A little bit . . .) (cf. p. 96)

Tsugoo-ga tsukimasen-node. (*lit.* Because I can't make it convenient.)

□implying impossibility

Ichioo yatte-mimasu-ga . . . (I'll try, but . . . — *lit.* I'll try it once.) (cf. p. 83)

Dekiru-dake-no koto-wa shimasu-ga . . . (I'll do my best, but . . . — *lit.* I'll do as much as I can, but . . .)

Doozo ashikarazu. (Please understand. — *lit.* Please don't feel bad.)

OFFERING
□help

Otetsudai-sasete-kudasai. (Let me help you.)

Yokattara otetsudai-shimasu. (I'll help you if it's all right.)

□giving presents

Tsumaranai mono-desu-ga . . . (It's very little, but . . . — *lit.* It's a trifling thing, but . . .) (cf. p. 125)

Honno sukoshi-desu-ga . . . (It's very little, but . . . — *lit.* It's only a little bit, but . . .)

Kokoro-bakari-no mono-desu-ga . . . (It's very little, but . . . — *lit.* It's nothing but my heart, but . . .)

□offering food

Doozo (meshiagatte-kudasai). (Please have some.) (cf. p.66)

Moo sukoshi ikaga-desu-ka. (Have some more, please. — *lit.* How about a little more?)

Gohan-no okawari-wa? (*lit.* How about another helping of rice?)

ACCEPTING
□presents

Arigatoo-gozaimasu. (Thank you very much.)

Konna mono itadaku wake-niwa ikimasen. (I shouldn't accept this.) (This can be just a formality. Usually the offer will be repeated until the present is accepted.)

□meals

Itadakimasu. (Thank you. — before one starts eating — *lit.* I'm going to receive it.) (cf. p. 54)

Gochisoosama-deshita. (Thank you. — when one has finished eating — *lit.* It was a feast.) (cf. p. 54)

□help

Sumimasen. Onegai-shimasu. (Thank you. Please do so.)

EXPRESSIONS WHEN VISITING
□by a visitor at the door

Gomen-kudasai. (Excuse me. Hello. — *lit.* Excuse me.)

Kono hen-made kimashita-node. (I just happened to be in the neighborhood. — *lit.* I came to this area, so . . .)

Chotto ojama-itashimasu. (Excuse me. — *lit.* I'm going to interrupt you a little bit — meaning "I'm going to stay a little while.")

□**by a host(ess) at the door**

Yoku irasshaimashita. (Welcome. — *lit.* You've come well.)

Doozo ohairi-kudasai. (Please come in.)

□**by a visitor to the host(ess) preparing something for him**

Doozo okamai-naku. Sugu shitsuree-shimasu-kara. (Please don't bother. I'll be leaving very soon.)

□**taking leave**

Sorosoro shitsuree-itashimasu. (It's about time I should be leaving.)

□**detaining the visitor**

Mada yoroshii-ja arimasen-ka. (Must you really leave so soon? — *lit.* Isn't it still all right?)

Doozo goyukkuri. (Please take your time.)

□**by a visitor when leaving**

Taihen ojama-itashimashita. (Thank you very much. I had a wonderful time. — *lit.* I interrupted you very much.) (cf. p. 68)

Gochisoosama-deshita. (Thank you. I had a very good time. — *lit.* Thank you for the feast.) (cf. p. 54)

□**by a host(ess) seeing the visitor off**

(Sekkaku oide-itadakimashita-noni) nanno okamai-mo dekimasen-de . . . (Thank you for coming. I'm sorry I couldn't do much to entertain you. — *lit.* I couldn't do much (although you took so much trouble to come).)

Zehi mata oide-kudasai. (Please come again. — *lit.* By all means please come again.)

157

INDEX TO WORDS, PHRASES AND SENTENCES